TOP NOTCH

English for Today's World

2

Joan Saslow ■ Allen Ascher

With *Top Notch Pop Songs and Karaoke*
by Rob Morsberger

PEARSON
Longman

Top Notch: English for Today's World 2

Pearson Education, 10 Bank Street, White Plains, NY 10606

Editorial director: Pamela Fishman
Senior development editor: Martin Yu
Vice president, director of design and production: Rhea Banker
Director of electronic production: Aliza Greenblatt
Managing editor: Mike Kemper
Art director: Ann France

Senior manufacturing buyer: Dave Dickey
Photo research: Aerin Csigay
Digital layout specialist: Warren Fischbach
Text composition: Kirchoff-Wohlberg
Text font: Palatino 11/13
Cover photograph: "From Above," by Rhea Banker.
Copyright © 2005 Rhea Banker.

4.3.2.1 CIP data was provided for the original edition

The Library of Congress has cataloged the earlier edition as follows:

Saslow, Joan M.
   Top notch : English for today's world. Student book. 2 / Joan Saslow, Allen Ascher.
      p. cm.
   1. English language—Textbooks for foreign speakers. 2. English language—Problems, exercises, etc. I. Ascher, Allen. II. Title.
PE1128.S2758 2006
428.2'4—dc22   2004048283

ISBNs: 0-13-184034-7 (pbk. :alk. paper)
   0-13-223044-5 (Student's Book with Take-Home Super CD-ROM)

Photo credits: All original photography by David Mager. page 2 (top left) Will & Deni McIntyre/Getty Images, (top middle left) Michael Goldman/Masterfile, (top middle right) Robert Frerck/Odyssey Productions, Inc., (right) Jeff Greenberg/PhotoEdit, (left middle) Michael Newman/PhotoEdit, (left middle left) Mark Hamilton/Dorling Kindersley; p. 3 David R. Frazier Photolibrary, Inc.; p. 5 (background) Luis Villota/Corbis, (left) Gary Conner/PhotoEdit, (top middle) Adam Woolfitt/Corbis, (bottom middle) David Sacks/Getty Images, (top right) Michal Heron, (bottom right) Bob Krist/eStock Photo; p. 6 (inset) Mathias Oppersdorff/Photo Researchers, Inc., (feijoada) Mourad Tarek/Stockfood America; p. 7 (left to right) Dallas & John Heaton/Corbis, Dallas & John Heaton/Corbis, John Neubauer/PhotoEdit, Renee Comet Photography/Stockfood America, Picture Finders Ltd./eStock Photo; p. 8 (middle) Garry Hunger/Getty Images; p. 11 (snake) Jerry Young/Dorling Kindersley, (octopus) Frank Greenaway/Dorling Kindersley, (pig) Mike Dunning/Dorling Kindersley, (cheese) Spencer Jones/Corbis, (Moscow) Jose Fuste Raga/eStock Photo, (Shanghai) Steve Vidler/eStock Photo, (Istanbul) John Henley/Corbis, (Honolulu) Vladpans/eStock Photo, (gliding) Sunstar/Photo Researchers, Inc., (sailing) Image du Sud/eStock Photo, (riding) Fritz Prenzel/Peter Arnold, Inc., (snorkeling) Norbert Wu/Peter Arnold, Inc.; p. 12 (upper top) Nik Wheeler/Corbis, (lower top) Gunter Marx Photography/Corbis, (bottom left to right) Renee Comet Photography/Stockfood America, SuperStock, Steve Vidler/eStock Photo, Tibor Bognar, Rafael Macia/Photo Researchers; p. 14 (background) Tom Daly/Getty Images, (top right) Photofest, (left) John Springer/Corbis, (bottom right) Royalty-Free/Corbis; p.15 (middle) www.comstock.com; p. 16 (bottom) Dave Parker/Alpha/Globe Photos; p. 17 (background) Graham Monro/Photolibrary.com, (bottom) Shaun Egan/Getty Images; p. 18 (action) Original Films/Bob Marshak/The Kobal Collection, (comedy) Morgan Creek/The Kobal Collection, (documentary) AP Wide World Photos, (drama) Paramount/The Kobal Collection, (horror) Warner Bros/The Kobal Collection, (musical) 20th Century Fox/The Kobal Collection, (sci-fi) MGM/The Kobal Collection, (animated) Globe Photos (bottom) Clive Streeter/Dorling Kindersley; p. 22 (left) Warner 7 Arts/The Kobal Collection, (right) Bettmann/Corbis; p. 23 Rob Melnychuk/Getty Images; p. 30 (background) Ron Brown/SuperStock, (single) Jeff Greenberg/PhotoEdit, (double) Jeff Greenberg/PhotoEdit; p. 32 (background) Andrew McKim/Masterfile, (towels) www.comstock.com, (hangers) Jose Luis Pelaez, Inc./Corbis, (iron) Michael Matisse/Getty Images, (dryer) Getty Images, (make up) Jeff Greenberg/Index Stock Imagery, (turn down) www.comstock.com, (bring up) David Bartruff Inc.; p. 33 Andy Crawford/Dorling Kindersley; p. 34 (left) Dorling Kindersley, (middle) Rudi Von Briel/PhotoEdit, (right) Bernard Boutrit/Woodfin Camp Associates; p. 38 (computer) Stockbyte, (bottom) Steve Gorton/Dorling Kindersley; p. 44 (background) Photolibrary.com, (sedan) Courtesy DaimlerChrysler Corporation, (wagon) Tim Ridley/Dorling Kindersley, (convertible) David Young-Wolff/PhotoEdit, (luxury) Ron Kimball Photography, (SUV) Kurt Wittman/Corbis, (van) David Young-Wolff/PhotoEdit, (compact) Greg Martin/SuperStock, (full) Ron Kimball/Ron Kimball Stock, (sports) Adam Woolfitt/Corbis; p. 46 (top right) Corbis Digital Stock, (steak) Renee Comet Photography/Stockfood America, (sardines) Maximilian Stock/Stockfood America, (shellfish) Geoffrey Clifford/Woodfin Camp Associates, (tofu) Gary Conner/PhotoEdit, (steak) Renee Comet Photography/Stockfood America, (noodles) Alan Campbell Productions/Stockfood America, (fries) Maximilian Stock/Stockfood America; p. 66 (sushi) Vito Arcomano/eStock Photo, (mango) Dorey Cardinale Photography/Stockfood America, (ice cream) Judd Pilossof/FoodPix, (pasta) Thom DeSanto Photography, Inc./Stockfood America, (asparagus) Andy Ryan Photography/Stockfood America; p. 68 Dave King/Dorling Kindersley; p. 69 Digital Vision Ltd.; p. 70 (A left) Cathy Melloan/PhotoEdit, (A right) Gary White Photography/Stockfood America, (B left) Jimmy Dorantes/LatinFocus.com, (B right) George D. Lepp/Corbis, (C) Steve Cohen/FoodPix, (D) David Young-Wolff/PhotoEdit, (E) Foodcollection/Stockfood America, (F) Michael Newman/PhotoEdit; p. 71 Stephen Hayward/Dorling Kindersley; p. 73 (background) Tyson Foods, Inc., (US) Spathias & Miller/Stockfood America, (China) John E. Kelly/FoodPix, (Brazil) Michael Newman/PhotoEdit, (Korea) James Baigrie/FoodPix, (Vietnam) Steven Mark Needham/FoodPix, (Venezuela) Renee Comet Photography/Stockfood America, (Mexico) Jimmy Dorantes/LatinFocus.com; p. 75 Bob Elsdale/Getty Images; p. 76 Photolibrary.com; p. 77 (top left to right) Leslye Borden/PhotoEdit, Troy Wayrynen/Columbian/NewSport/Corbis, eStock Photo, Corbis Digital Stock, (middle left to right) Setboun/Corbis, Corbis Digital Stock, Neal & Molly Jansen/SuperStock, Image Source/ImageState; p. 79 Dorling Kindersley; p. 80 David Butlow/Corbis; p. 81 (top) David Muir/Masterfile, (bottom) Getty Images; p. 83 (top) Jerry Tobias/Corbis, (left) Tony Freeman/PhotoEdit, (right) Anthony Redpath/Corbis, (bottom) Ken Weingart/ImageState; p. 86 (Top left) Historical Picture Archive/Corbis, (bottom left) O'Keeffe, Georgia (1887-1986). "White Flower on Red Earth, #1". 1943. Oil on canvas, 26" x 30 1/4". Inv.: 46.157. The Newark Museum/Art Resource, NY; p. 88 Francis G. Mayer/Corbis; p. 89 (Accademia) Alinari Archives/Corbis, (David) Copyright © 2001 by Martin Yu, (Palace) Bohemian Nomad Picturemakers/Corbis, (Kuan) Fan Kuan, Chinese. Travelers among Mountains and Streams, c. 1000. Hanging scroll, ink and colors on silk, 81 1/4 " L. Collection of the National Palace Museum, Taiwan, Republic of China, (Louvre) Richard List/Corbis, (da Vinci) Gianni Dagli Orti/Corbis; p. 90 (glass) Susan Van Etten/PhotoEdit, (silver) Charles Edensaw (c. 1839-1924). Silver bracelet (eagle design), c. 1890. Coin silver. Native American, Haida. Diam. 2 1/2 "; H. 1 3/16". Accession number 91.1.130. Gift of John H. Hauberg. Photograph by Paul Macapia. Seattle Art Museum, (gold) Art Resource, NY, (clay) Stockbyte, (wood) Heini Schneebeli/The Bridgeman Art Library International Ltd., (stone) Corbis, (cloth) Keren Su/Corbis, (chair) Victoria & Albert Museum, London/Art Resource, NY, (figure) The Art Archive/Egyptian Museum Turin/Jacqueline Hyde/Picture Desk, (vase) The Art Archive/Museo Vetriano de Murano/Dagli Orti(A)/Picture Desk, (bowl) Banco Mexicano de Imaagenes/The Bridgeman Art Library International Ltd., (bag) David Young-Wolff/PhotoEdit, (figure) Sakamoto Photo Research Laboratory/Corbis; p. 91 (dolls) Dave G. Houser/Corbis, (vase Korea) Corbis, (gold figure) Mireille Vautier/Woodfin Camp & Associates, (vase France) The Art Archive/Dagli Orti(A)/Picture Desk, (stone figure) Claudia Obrocki/Art Resource, NY, (wood figure) Dave G. Houser/Corbis; p. 92 Photos of Yu Gan, Yu Heng, and Yu Kuai courtesy of Yu Gan; p. 93 Dorling Kindersley; p. 94 (background) Marcel Bekken/Fotopersbureau Noordoost, (portrait) Giraudon/Art Resource, (Arles) Damir Frkovic/Masterfile, (vase) Art Resource, NY; p. 95 (Rodin) Hulton Archive/Getty Images, (Lee) Reuters NewMedia Inc./Corbis, (Versace) Rune Hellestad/Corbis, (brush) Tim Ridley/Dorling Kindersley, (Salgado) Vincenzo Pinto/Corbis, (Cassat) Culver Pictures, Inc., (Gehry) AP Wide World Photos; p. 96 (A) Collier Campbell Lifeworks/Corbis, (B) Archivo Iconografico, S.A./Corbis, (keyboard) Corbis Digital Stock, (C) Art Resource, NY, (D) Art Resource, (E) The Art Archive/Museo del Oro Bogota/Dagli Orti(A)/Picture Desk, (F) Erich Lessing/Art Resource, NY; p. 97 (background) Chris Orr/Dorling Kindersley, (National) Wolfgang Kaehler/Corbis, (Eyck) Jan van Eyck (c. 1390-1441), The Portrait of Giovanni, Arnolfini and his Wife Giovanna Cenami. The Arnolfini Marriage, 1434 oil on panel. National Gallery, London, UK/Bridgeman Art Library, (Victoria) Sandro Vannini/Corbis, (Luck) Art Resource, NY, (Tate) Paul Solomon/Woodfin Camp & Associates, (British) Macduff Everton/Corbis, (Mustard) Roy Lichtenstein, Mustard on White. 1963. Magnacolour on plexiglass. 80 x 94 x 5.1 cm. Lent from a private collection. Tate Gallery, London. (c) Tate Gallery, London / Art Resource, NY. (c) Estate of Roy Lichtenstein, (Discus) Scala/Art Resource, NY; p. 98 (monitor) Burke/Triolo/Getty Images, (mic) Getty Images, (head) Logitech, Inc., (speakers) Logitech, Inc., (drive) Corbis Digital Stock, (keyboard) Logitech, Inc., (games) Frank LaBua/Pearson Education/PH College, (joy) Logitech, Inc., (soft) Frank LaBua/Pearson Education/PH College; p. 99 Courtesy Epson America, Inc. & Mercier Wimberg Photography; p. 100 Images.com/Corbis; p. 101 Logitech, Inc.; p. 103 PalmOne, Inc.; p. 105 Nicholas Eveleigh/SuperStock; p. 110 (middle) Getty Images; p. 111 Richard Cummins/Corbis; p. 113 (wallet) Steve Gorton/Dorling Kindersley, (glove) Clive Streeter/Dorling Kindersley, (jacket) Steve Gorton & Andy Crawford/Dorling Kindersley, (suitcase) Dorling Kindersley, (phone) Dorling Kindersley, (books) Myrleen Ferguson Cate/PhotoEdit; p. 116 (top) Robert Rathe/Mira.com, (middle) Catherine Karnow/Corbis, (bottom) Jeffrey Allan Salter/Corbis; p. 117 Library of Congress; p. 118 (background) Ken Ross/Getty Images.

Illustration credits: Steve Attoe, pp. 6, 24, 66, 82, 104, 111; Sue Carlson, p. 35; John Ceballos, pp. 10, 25, 37, 49, 61, 85, 109, 121; Mark Collins, pp. 27, 42, 87; John Hovell, pp. 9, 46; Brian Hughes, pp. 15, 22, 40, 41, 42, 47, 55, 62, 71, 118; Andy Myer, pp. 17, 64, 106; Dusan Petricic, pp. 8, 33, 41, 70, 78, 79, 115; Jake Rickwood, p. 20; Neil Stewart, pp. 50, 119; Anne Veltfort, pp. 31, 54; Jean Wisenbaugh, p. 13.

Printed in the United States of America
9 10–QWD –10 09 08

Contents

Scope and Sequence OF CONTENT AND SKILLS

GRAMMAR BOOSTER

UNIT	Vocabulary*	Conversation Strategies	Grammar	
1 **Greetings and Small Talk** Page 2 *Top Notch* Song: "Greetings and Small Talk"	• Customs around the world • Tourist activities	• Ask <u>What have you been up to?</u> or <u>How have you been?</u> to start a conversation • Add information beyond <u>Yes</u> or <u>No</u> to continue a conversation • Use <u>That's great</u> to shift to a new topic	• The present perfect: <u>yet</u>, <u>already</u>, <u>ever</u>, and <u>before</u> • past participles	• Further explanation of form and usage: the present perfect
2 **Movies and Entertainment** Page 14 *Top Notch* Song: "Better Late Than Never"	• Explanations for being late • Ways to express likes and dislikes • Movie genres • Adjectives to describe movies	• Use <u>They say</u> to support a suggestion • Use <u>Actually</u> to indicate that what you are about to say may be surprising • Use <u>For real?</u> to convey surprise	• The present perfect: additional uses—<u>for</u> and <u>since</u> • <u>Would rather</u>	• Contrasting the present perfect and the present perfect continuous • Spelling rules for the present participle
3 **Staying at Hotels** Page 26	• Telephone messages • Hotel room features • Hotel facilities • Hotel room amenities and services	• Use <u>I'd like to</u> to politely state your purpose on the phone • Use <u>That's right</u> to confirm • Use <u>By the way</u> to introduce a new topic or a question	• The future with <u>will</u> • <u>Had better</u>	• Further explanation of usage: future with <u>will</u> and <u>be going to</u> • Degrees of obligation: <u>have to</u>, <u>must</u>, <u>had better</u>, <u>be supposed to</u>, <u>should</u>, <u>ought to</u>, and <u>could</u>
4 **Cars and Driving** Page 38 *Top Notch* Song: "Wheels around the World"	• Ways to show concern • Car parts • Types of cars • Bad driving behaviors • Polite address • Phrasal verbs	• Use expressions such as <u>I'm so sorry</u> and <u>How awful</u> to convey concern • Begin a response with <u>Well</u> to introduce an explanation	• The past continuous • Direct object placement with phrasal verbs	• Further explanation of usage: the past continuous • Direct object placement: separable and inseparable phrasal verbs
5 **Personal Care and Appearance** Page 50	• Personal care products • Salon services • Ways to schedule and pay for personal care • Ways to improve appearance	• Repeat part of a question before answering to clarify • Use <u>Can I get</u> to make a request more polite	• Count and non-count nouns: indefinite quantities and amounts—<u>some</u>, <u>any</u>, <u>a lot of</u>, <u>many</u>, and <u>much</u> • <u>Someone</u> and <u>anyone</u>	• Review of non-count nouns: containers, quantifiers, and other modifiers • <u>Too many</u>, <u>too much</u>, and <u>enough</u> • Indefinite pronouns: <u>something</u>, <u>anything</u>, and <u>nothing</u>

*In *Top Notch*, the term *vocabulary* refers to individual words, phrases, and expressions.

Speaking	Pronunciation	Listening	Reading	Writing
• Offer to introduce someone • Get reacquainted with someone • Greet a visitor • Talk about tourist activities • Explain local customs • Ask about life experiences	• Negative contractions	• People ask visitors about what they've done Task: identify activities • A game show Task: describe the guests' life experiences • Conversation with a visitor Task: identify tourist sights visited	• Magazine article about gestures around the world • Customs around the world • Experiences survey	• Write about an experience • Create a guide for visitors to your country on how to behave • Introduce yourself
• Apologize for and explain lateness • Offer to pay or return the favor • Compare tastes in movies • Describe movies you've seen lately • Discuss the effects of violence in the media	• Reduction of /h/	• Movie reviews Task: identify genres and recommendations • Two people choose a movie to see Task: write movie descriptions • Conversations about movies Task: use adjectives to describe the movies	• Magazine article about violence in movies • Movie catalog ads • Movie reviews	• Write a movie review page • Express opinions about violence in media
• Leave and take a phone message • Check into and out of a hotel • Discuss hotel room features and facilities • Request housekeeping services • Choose a hotel	• Contractions with will	• Phone calls to a hotel Task: take phone messages • Conversations about hotel reservations Task: write the room features guests want • Requests for hotel room amenities and services Task: identify the services and items requested	• Tourist guide recommending New York hotels • Hotel bill • Hotel preference survey	• Describe the advantages and disadvantages of a hotel • Describe a hotel you've stayed at
• Describe a car accident and damage • Express concern • Ask for service and repairs • Describe car problems • Rent a car • Discuss driving rules	• Stress of particles in phrasal verbs	• People describe car accidents Task: identify car damage • Phone calls to a car rental agency Task: infer if the caller rented the car • Conversations with a car rental agent Task: listen for car types	• Magazine article about driving abroad • Online response to car rental request • International road signs • Driving safety survey	• Compare good and bad drivers
• Shop for personal care products • Ask for something you can't find • Request salon services • Schedule and pay for personal care • Discuss ways people improve their appearance	• Vowel reduction to /ə/	• Radio advertisements Task: identify personal care products • Conversations about salon appointments Task: identify salon services • Customers ask about personal care services Task: listen for the services requested and explain what happened	• Advice column about cosmetic surgery • Personal appearance survey	• Write a letter to a magazine's editor • Describe a personal care product you like

Scope and Sequence OF CONTENT AND SKILLS

GRAMMAR BOOSTER

UNIT	Vocabulary	Conversation Strategies	Grammar	
6 **Eating Well** *Page 62*	• Excuses for not eating something • Food passions • Lifestyles and health problems • Describing food	• Use <u>Don't worry about it</u> to decline an apology • Use <u>Well</u> to introduce an opinion that differs from someone else's	• Negative <u>yes</u> / <u>no</u> questions and <u>Why don't</u> …? • <u>Used to</u>	• Further explanation of usage: negative <u>yes</u> / <u>no</u> questions with short answers • Further explanation of usage: <u>Why don't</u> / <u>doesn't</u> …? • Further explanation of form: <u>used to</u>
7 **Psychology and Personality** *Page 74* *Top Notch* Song: "The Colors of Love"	• Describing colors • Adjectives of emotion • Suggestions to cheer someone up • Adjectives to describe personality	• Use <u>You know,</u>... to be less abrupt • Use <u>out of the question</u> to indicate opposition • Use <u>Really?</u> to indicate a difference of opinion • Use <u>Thanks for asking</u> to acknowledge another's concern	• Gerunds and infinitives after certain verbs • Gerunds after prepositions • Expressions with prepositions	• Further explanation of form and usage: gerunds and infinitives • Negative gerunds
8 **Enjoying the Arts** *Page 86* *Top Notch* Song: "To Each His Own"	• Types of art • Common materials • Positive adjectives • Ways to say you don't like something	• Use <u>For one thing</u> to provide one reason among several • Use <u>Excuse me</u> to ask for attention in a store	• The passive voice: statements and questions	• Further explanation of form and usage: the passive voice • The passive voice: intransitive verbs
9 **Living with Computers** *Page 98*	• Computer products and accessories • Computer toolbars and commands • Internet activities	• Use <u>Oh yeah?</u> to show that you are interested • Use <u>Everyone says</u> to solicit an opinion • Use <u>Well</u> to soften a contradictory opinion • Use <u>Why don't you</u> to respectfully offer advice	• Comparisons with <u>as … as</u> • The infinitive of purpose	• Review: comparatives and superlatives • <u>As … as</u> with adverbs • Expressing purpose with <u>in order to</u> and <u>for</u>
10 **Ethics and Values** *Page 110*	• Ways to acknowledge thanks • Ways to express certainty • Moral dilemmas • Personal values	• Use <u>Excuse me</u> to get a stranger's attention • Ask <u>You think so?</u> to probe the wisdom of a course of action	• Possessive pronouns • Factual and unreal conditional sentences	• Further explanation of form and usage: factual and unreal conditional sentences

Speaking	Pronunciation	Listening	Reading	Writing
• Offer dishes and decline food • Talk about foods you love and hate • Discuss lifestyle changes • Describe unique foods	• <u>Used to</u>	• Conversations about food <u>Task</u>: identify excuses for not eating something • Descriptions of food passions <u>Task</u>: determine each person's food passions • Descriptions of unique foods <u>Task</u>: describe food items	• News article about changing lifestyles and obesity • The healthy-eating pyramid • Lifestyle survey	• Write about lifestyle changes • Describe a dish
• State color preferences • Describe your mood and emotions • Cheer someone up • Discuss personatlity types • Discuss the impact of birth order on relationships	• Reduction of <u>to</u> in infinitive phrases	• Conversations about color preferences <u>Task</u>: write color names and adjectives of emotion • An academic lecture <u>Task</u>: infer definitions of personality • Conversations about emotions <u>Task</u>: describe how each speaker feels about certain things	• Magazine article about the impact of birth order on personality • Color survey • Personality survey	• Describe your own personality • Describe the personality of someone you know well
• Recommend a museum • Describe an object • Describe how you decorate your home • Discuss your favorite artists • Express opinions about art	• Emphatic stress	• A biography of Vincent Van Gogh <u>Task</u>: listen for his life events • Conversations about art objects <u>Task</u>: identify the objects discussed	• Magazine article about the role of art in two people's lives • Guide to London museums	• Create a short biography of an artist you like • Describe a piece of art you like
• Discuss buying a computer product • Recommend "a better deal" • Troubleshoot a problem • Describe how you use computers • Discuss the benefits and problems of the Internet	• Stress in <u>as … as</u> phrases	• Conversations about using computers <u>Task</u>: identify computer commands • Descriptions of computer activities <u>Task</u>: listen for things to do on the Internet • Conversations comparing two computer products <u>Task</u>: complete comparative sentences	• Four news articles about serious problems with the Internet • Electronics store website • Consumer information card	• Express your opinion about the social impact of the Internet • Report how you use a computer
• Return lost property • Discuss an ethical choice • Express personal values • Discuss honesty • Warn about consequences	• Assimilation of the sounds /d/ + /y/	• Conversations about personal values <u>Task</u>: identify each person's personal values and infer meaning of key words and phrases	• News article about the Tokyo lost-and-found • Values self-test	• Express opinions about modesty • Write an article about appropriate appearance in your country • Narrate a true story about an ethical choice

Acknowledgments

Top Notch International Advisory Board

The authors gratefully acknowledge the substantive and formative contributions of the members of the International Advisory Board.

CHERYL BELL, Middlesex County College, Middlesex, New Jersey, USA • **ELMA CABAHUG**, City College of San Francisco, San Francisco, California, USA • **JO CARAGATA**, Mukogawa Women's University, Hyogo, Japan • **ANN CARTIER**, Palo Alto Adult School, Palo Alto, California, USA • **TERRENCE FELLNER**, Himeji Dokkyo University, Hyogo, Japan • **JOHN FUJIMORI**, Meiji Gakuin High School, Tokyo, Japan • **ARETA ULHANA GALAT**, Escola Superior de Estudos Empresariais e Informática, Curitiba, Brazil • **DOREEN M. GAYLORD**, Kanazawa Technical College, Ishikawa, Japan • **EMILY GEHRMAN**, Newton International College, Garden Grove, California, USA • **ANN-MARIE HADZIMA**, National Taiwan University, Taipei, Taiwan • **KAREN KYONG-AI PARK**, Seoul National University, Seoul, Korea • **ANA PATRICIA MARTÍNEZ VITE DIP. R.S.A.**, Universidad del Valle de México, Mexico City, Mexico • **MICHELLE ANN MERRITT, PROULEX/** Universidad de Guadalajara, Guadalajara, Mexico • **ADRIANNE P. OCHOA**, Georgia State University, Atlanta, Georgia, USA • **LOUIS PARDILLO**, Korea Herald English Institute, Seoul, Korea • **THELMA PERES**, Casa Thomas Jefferson, Brasilia, Brazil • **DIANNE RUGGIERO**, Broward Community College, Davie, Florida, USA • **KEN SCHMIDT**, Tohoku Fukushi University, Sendai, Japan • **ALISA A. TAKEUCHI**, Garden Grove Adult Education, Garden Grove, California, USA • **JOSEPHINE TAYLOR**, Centro Colombo Americano, Bogotá, Colombia • **PATRICIA VECIÑO**, Instituto Cultural Argentino Norteamericano, Buenos Aires, Argentina • **FRANCES WESTBROOK**, AUA Language Center, Bangkok, Thailand

Reviewers and Piloters

Many thanks also to the reviewers and piloters all over the world who reviewed *Top Notch* in its final form.

G. Julian Abaqueta, Huachiew Chalermprakiet University, Samutprakarn, Thailand • **David Aline**, Kanagawa University, Kanagawa, Japan • **Marcia Alves**, Centro Cultural Brasil Estados Unidos, Franca, Brazil • **Yousef Al-Yacoub**, Qatar Petroleum, Doha, Qatar • **Maristela Barbosa Silveira e Silva**, Instituto Cultural Brasil-Estados Unidos, Manaus, Brazil • **Beth Bartlett**, Centro Colombo Americano, Cali, Colombia • **Carla Battigelli**, University of Zulia, Maracaibo, Venezuela • **Claudia Bautista**, C.B.C., Caracas, Venezuela • **Rob Bell**, Shumei Yachiyo High School, Chiba, Japan • **Dr. Maher Ben Moussa**, Sharjah University, Sharjah, United Arab Emirates • **Elaine Cantor**, Englewood Senior High School, Jacksonville, Florida, USA • **María Aparecida Capellari**, SENAC, São Paulo, Brazil • **Eunice Carrillo Ramos**, Colegio Durango, Naucalpan, Mexico • **Janette Carvalhinho de Oliveira**, Centro de Linguas (UFES), Vitória, Brazil • **María Amelia Carvalho Fonseca**, Centro Cultural Brasil-Estados Unidos, Belém, Brazil • **Audy Castañeda**, Instituto Pedagógico de Caracas, Caracas, Venezuela • **Ching-Fen Chang**, National Chiao Tung University, Hsinchu, Taiwan • **Ying-Yu Chen**, Chinese Culture University, Taipei, Taiwan • **Joyce Chin**, The Language Training and Testing Center, Taipei, Taiwan • **Eun Cho**, Pagoda Language School, Seoul, Korea • **Hyungzung Cho**, MBC Language Institute, Seoul, Korea • **Dong Sua Choi**, MBC Language Institute, Seoul, Korea • **Jeong Mi Choi**, Freelancer, Seoul, Korea • **Peter Chun**, Pagoda Language School, Seoul, Korea • **Eduardo Corbo**, Legacy ELT, Salto, Uruguay • **Marie Cosgrove**, Surugadai University, Saitama, Japan • **María Antonieta Covarrubias Souza**, Centro Escolar Akela, Mexico City, Mexico • **Katy Cox**, Casa Thomas Jefferson, Brasilia, Brazil • **Michael Donovan**, Gakushuin University, Tokyo, Japan • **Stewart Dorward**, Shumei Eiko High School, Saitama, Japan • **Ney Eric Espina**, Centro Venezolano Americano del Zulia, Maracaibo, Venezuela • **Edith Espino**, Centro Especializado de Lenguas - Universidad Tecnológica de Panamá, El Dorado, Panama • **Allen P. Fermon**, Instituto Brasil-Estados Unidos, Ceará, Brazil • **Simão Ferreira Banha**, Phil Young's English School, Curitiba, Brazil • **María Elena Flores Lara**, Colegio Mercedes, Mexico City, Mexico • **Valesca Fróis Nassif**, Associação Cultural Brasil-Estados Unidos, Salvador, Brazil • **José Fuentes**, Empire Language Consulting, Caracas, Venezuela • **José Luis Guerrero**, Colegio Cristóbal Colón, Mexico City, Mexico • **Claudia Patricia Gutiérrez**, Centro Colombo Americano, Cali, Colombia • **Valerie Hansford**, Asia University, Tokyo, Japan • **Gene Hardstark**, Dotkyo University, Saitama, Japan • **Maiko Hata**, Kansai University, Osaka, Japan • **Susan Elizabeth Haydock Miranda de Araujo**, Centro Cultural Brasil Estados Unidos, Belém, Brazil • **Gabriela Herrera**, Fundametal, Valencia, Venezuela • **Sandy Ho**, GEOS International, New York, New York, USA • **Yuri Hosoda**, Showa Women's University, Tokyo, Japan • **Hsiao-I Hou**, Shu-Te University, Kaohsiung County, Taiwan • **Kuei-ping Hsu**, National Tsing Hua University, Hsinchu, Taiwan • **Chia-yu Huang**, National Tsing Hua University, Hsinchu, Taiwan • **Caroline C. Hwang**, National Taipei University of Science and Technology, Taipei, Taiwan • **Diana Jones**, Angloamericano, Mexico City, Mexico • **Eunjeong Kim**, Freelancer, Seoul, Korea • **Julian Charles King**, Qatar Petroleum, Doha, Qatar • **Bruce Lee**, CIE: Foreign Language Institute, Seoul, Korea • **Myunghee Lee**, MBC Language Institute, Seoul, Korea • **Naidnapa Leoprasertkul**, Language Development Center, Mahasarakham University, Mahasarakham, Thailand • **Eleanor S. Leu**, Souchow University, Taipei, Taiwan • **Eliza Liu**, Chinese Culture University, Taipei, Taiwan • **Carlos Lizárraga**, Angloamericano, Mexico City, Mexico • **Philippe Loussarevian**, Keio University Shonan Fujisawa High School, Kanagawa, Japan • **Jonathan Lynch**, Azabu University, Tokyo, Japan • **Thomas Mach**, Konan University, Hyogo, Japan • **Lilian Mandel Civatti**, Associação Cultural Brasil-Estados Unidos, Salvador, Brazil • **Hakan Mansuroglu**, Zoni Language Center, West New York, New Jersey, USA • **Martha McGaughey**, Language Training Institute, Englewood Cliffs, New Jersey, USA • **David Mendoza Plascencia**, Instituto Internacional de Idiomas, Naucalpan, Mexico • **Theresa Mezo**, Interamerican University, Río Piedras, Puerto Rico • **Luz Adriana Montenegro Silva**, Colegio CAFAM, Bogotá, Colombia • **Magali de Moraes Menti**, Instituto Lingua, Porto Alegre, Brazil • **Massoud Moslehpour**, The Overseas Chinese Institute of Technology, Taichung, Taiwan • **Jennifer Nam**, IKE, Seoul, Korea • **Marcos Norelle F. Victor**, Instituto Brasil-Estados Unidos, Ceará, Brazil • **Luz María Olvera**, Instituto Juventud del Estado de México, Naucalpan, Mexico • **Roxana Orrego Ramírez**, Universidad Diego Portales, Santiago, Chile • **Ming-Jong Pan**, National Central University, Jhongli City, Taiwan • **Sandy Park**, Topia Language School, Seoul, Korea • **Patrícia Elizabeth Peres Martins**, Instituto Brasil-Estados Unidos, Rio de Janeiro, Brazil • **Rodrigo Peza**, Passport Language Centers, Bogotá, Colombia • **William Porter**, Osaka Institute of Technology, Osaka, Japan • **Caleb Prichard**, Kwansei Gakuin University, Hyogo, Japan • **Mirna Quintero**, Instituto Pedagógico de Caracas, Caracas, Venezuela • **Roberto Rabbini**, Seigakuin University, Saitama, Japan • **Terri Rapoport**, Berkeley College, White Plains, New York, USA • **Yvette Rieser**, Centro Electrónico de Idiomas, Maracaibo, Venezuela • **Orlando Rodríguez**, New English Teaching School, Paysandu, Uruguay • **Mayra Rosario**, Pontificia Universidad Católica Madre y Maestra, Santiago, Dominican Republic • **Peter Scout**, Sakura no Seibo Junior College, Fukushima, Japan • **Jungyeon Shim**, EG School, Seoul, Korea • **Keum Ok Song**, MBC Language Institute, Seoul, Korea • **Assistant Professor Dr. Reongrudee Soonthornmanee**, Chulalongkorn University Language Institute, Bangkok, Thailand • **Claudia Stanisclause**, The Language College, Maracay, Venezuela • **Tom Suh**, The Princeton Review, Seoul, Korea • **Phiphawin Suphawat**, KhonKaen University, KhonKaen, Thailand • **Craig Sweet**, Poole Gakuin Junior and Senior High Schools, Osaka, Japan • **Yi-nien Josephine Twu**, National Tsing Hua University, Hsinchu, Taiwan • **Maria Christina Uchôa Close**, Instituto Cultural Brasil-Estados Unidos, São José dos Campos, Brazil • **Luz Vanegas Lopera**, Lexicom The Place For Learning English, Medellín, Colombia • **Julieta Vasconcelos García**, Centro Escolar del Lago, A.C., Mexico City, Mexico • **Carol Vaughan**, Kanto Kokusai High School, Tokyo, Japan • **Patricia Celia Veciño**, Instituto Cultural Argentino Norteamericano, Buenos Aires, Argentina • **Isabela Villas Boas**, Casa Thomas Jefferson, Brasilia, Brazil • **Iole Vitti**, Peanuts English School, Poços de Caldas, Brazil • **Gabi Witthaus**, Qatar Petroleum, Doha, Qatar • **Yi-Ling Wu**, Shih Chien University, Taipei, Taiwan • **Chad Wynne**, Osaka Keizai University, Osaka, Japan • **Belkis Yanes**, Freelance Instructor, Caracas, Venezuela • **I-Chieh Yang**, Chung-kuo Institute of Technology, Taipei, Taiwan • **Emil Ysona**, Instituto Cultural Dominico-Americano, Santo Domingo, Dominican Republic • **Chi-fang Yu**, Soo Chow University, Taipei, Taiwan, • **Shigeki Yusa**, Sendai Shirayuri Women's College, Sendai, Japan

To the Teacher

What is *Top Notch*?

- *Top Notch* is a six-level communicative English course for adults and young adults, with two beginning entry levels.
- *Top Notch* prepares students to interact successfully and confidently with both native and non-native speakers of English.
- *Top Notch* demonstrably brings students to a "Top Notch" level of communicative competence.

Key Elements of the *Top Notch* Instructional Design

Concise two-page lessons

Each easy-to-teach two-page lesson is designed for one class session and begins with a clearly stated communication goal and ends with controlled or free communication practice. Each lesson provides vocabulary, grammar, and social language contextualized in all four skills, keeping the pace of a class session lively and varied.

Daily confirmation of progress

Adult and young adult students need to observe and confirm their own progress. In *Top Notch*, students conclude each class session with a controlled or free practice activity that demonstrates their ability to use new vocabulary, grammar, and social language. This motivates and keeps students eager to continue their study of English and builds their pride in being able to speak accurately, fluently, and authentically.

Real language

Carefully exposing students to authentic, natural English, both receptively and productively, is a necessary component of building understanding and expression. All conversation models feature the language people really use; nowhere to be found is "textbook English" written merely to exemplify grammar.

Practical content

In addition to classic topical vocabulary, grammar, and conversation, *Top Notch* includes systematic practice of highly practical language, such as: how to leave and take a phone message, how to request services at a hotel, how to make excuses to decline food you don't like, how to recommend a better deal—usable language today's students want and need.

Memorable model conversations

Effective language instruction must make language memorable. The full range of social and functional communicative needs is presented through practical model conversations that are intensively practiced and manipulated, first within a guided model and then in freer and more personalized formats.

High-impact vocabulary syllabus

In order to ensure students' solid acquisition of vocabulary essential for communication, *Top Notch* contains explicit presentation, practice, and systematic extended recycling of words, collocations, and expressions appropriate at each level of study. The extensive captioned illustrations, photos, definitions, examples, and contextualized sentences remove doubts about meaning and provide a permanent in-book reference for student test preparation. An added benefit is that teachers don't have to search for pictures to bring to class and don't have to resort to translating vocabulary into the students' native language.

Learner-supportive grammar

Grammar is approached explicitly and cognitively, through form, meaning, and use—both within the Student's Book units and in a bound-in Grammar Booster. Charts provide examples and paradigms enhanced by simple usage notes at students' level of comprehension. This takes the guesswork out of meaning, makes lesson preparation easier for teachers, and provides students with comprehensible charts for permanent reference and test preparation. All presentations of grammar are followed by exercises to ensure adequate practice.

English as an international language

Top Notch prepares students for interaction with both native and non-native speakers of English, both linguistically and culturally. English is treated as an international language, rather than the language of a particular country or region. In addition, *Top Notch* helps students develop a cultural fluency by creating an awareness of the varied rules across cultures for: politeness, greetings and introductions, appropriateness of dress in different settings, conversation do's and taboos, table manners, and other similar issues.

Two beginning-level texts

Beginning students can be placed either in *Top Notch 1* or *Top Notch Fundamentals*, depending on ability and background. Even absolute beginners can start with confidence in *Top Notch Fundamentals*. False beginners can begin with *Top Notch 1*. The *Top Notch Placement Test* clarifies the best placement within the series.

Estimated teaching time

Each level of *Top Notch* is designed for 60 to 90 instructional hours and contains a full range of supplementary components and enrichment devices to tailor the course to individual needs.

Components of *Top Notch 2*

Student's Book with Take-Home Super CD-ROM

The Super CD-ROM includes a variety of exciting interactive activities: Speaking Practice, Interactive Workbook, Games and Puzzles, and *Top Notch Pop* Karaoke. The disk can also be played on an audio CD player to listen to the Conversation Models and the *Top Notch Pop* songs.

Teacher's Edition and Lesson Planner

Complete yet concise lesson plans are provided for each class. Corpus notes provide essential information from the *Longman Spoken American Corpus* and the *Longman Learner's Corpus*. In addition, a free *Teacher's Resource Disk* offers the following printable extension activities to personalize your teaching style:
- Grammar self-checks
- *Top Notch Pop* song activities
- Writing process worksheets
- Learning strategies
- Pronunciation activities and supplements
- Extra reading comprehension activities
- Vocabulary cards and cumulative vocabulary activities
- Graphic organizers
- Pair work cards

Copy & Go: Ready-made Interactive Activities for Busy Teachers

Interactive games, puzzles, and other practice activities in convenient photocopiable form support the Student's Book content and provide a welcome change of pace.

Complete Classroom Audio Program

The audio program contains listening comprehension activities, rhythm and intonation practice, and targeted pronunciation activities that focus on accurate and comprehensible pronunciation.

Because *Top Notch* prepares students for international communication, a variety of native *and* non-native speakers are included to ready students for the world outside the classroom. The audio program also includes the five *Top Notch Pop* songs in standard and karaoke form.

Workbook

A tightly linked illustrated Workbook contains exercises that provide additional practice and reinforcement of language concepts and skills from *Top Notch* and its Grammar Booster.

Complete Assessment Package with *ExamView*® Software

Ten easy-to-administer and easy-to-score unit achievement tests assess listening, vocabulary, grammar, social language, reading, and writing. Two review tests, one mid-book and one end-of-book, provide additional cumulative assessment. Two speaking tests assess progress in speaking. In addition to the photocopiable achievement tests, *ExamView*® software enables teachers to tailor-make tests to best meet their needs by combining items in any way they wish.

Top Notch TV

A lively and entertaining video offers a TV-style situation comedy that reintroduces language from each *Top Notch* unit, plus authentic unrehearsed interviews with English speakers from around the world and authentic karaoke. Packaged with the video are activity worksheets and a booklet with teaching suggestions and complete video scripts.

Companion Website

A Companion Website at www.longman.com/topnotch provides numerous additional resources for students and teachers. This no-cost, high-benefit feature includes opportunities for further practice of language and content from the *Top Notch* Student's Book.

Welcome to Top Notch!

About the Authors

Joan Saslow

Joan Saslow has taught English as a Foreign Language and English as a Second Language to adults and young adults in both South America and the United States. She taught English and French at the Binational Centers of Valparaíso and Viña del Mar, Chile, and the Catholic University of Valparaíso. In the United States, Ms. Saslow taught English as a Foreign Language to Japanese university students at Marymount College and to international students in Westchester Community College's intensive English program as well as workplace English at the General Motors auto assembly plant in Tarrytown, NY.

Ms. Saslow is the series director of Longman's popular five-level adult series *True Colors: An EFL Course for Real Communication* and of *True Voices*, a five-level video course. She is author of *Ready to Go: Language, Lifeskills, and Civics*, a four-level adult ESL series; *Workplace Plus*, a vocational English series; and of *Literacy Plus*, a two-level series that teaches literacy, English, and culture to adult pre-literate students. She is also author of *English in Context: Reading Comprehension for Science and Technology*, a three-level series for English for special purposes. In addition, Ms. Saslow has been an author, an editor of language teaching materials, a teacher-trainer, and a frequent speaker at gatherings of EFL and ESL teachers for over thirty years.

Allen Ascher

Allen Ascher has been a teacher and teacher-trainer in both China and the United States, as well as an administrator and a publisher. Mr. Ascher specialized in teaching listening and speaking to students at the Beijing Second Foreign Language Institute, to hotel workers at a major international hotel in China, and to Japanese students from Chubu University studying English at Ohio University. In New York, Mr. Ascher taught students of all language backgrounds and abilities at the City University of New York, and he trained teachers in the TESOL Certificate Program at the New School. He was also the academic director of the International English Language Institute at Hunter College.

Mr. Ascher has provided lively workshops for EFL teachers throughout Asia, Latin America, Europe, and the Middle East. He is author of the popular *Think about Editing: A Grammar Editing Guide for ESL Writers*. As a publisher, Mr. Ascher played a key role in the creation of some of the most widely used materials for adults, including: *True Colors, NorthStar, Focus on Grammar, Global Links*, and *Ready to Go*. Mr. Ascher has an M.A. in Applied Linguistics from Ohio University.

Greetings and Small Talk

UNIT GOALS

1 Get reacquainted with someone
2 Greet a visitor to your country
3 Explain local customs
4 Ask about a person's experiences

 TOPIC PREVIEW. Look at the pictures. Do any of the pictures show behavior that would be unusual or strange in your country?

Customs Around the World

Greetings

bow

shake hands

kiss

hug

Exchanging business cards

with two hands

with one hand

Addressing people

Please call me Bill.

Hi, Bill. Call me Pam.

use first names

Hi. I'm Mrs. Song.

I'm Mr. Pike.

use last names

Small talk

So how much money do you make?

ask about salary

So how old are you?

ask about age

So how's your wife?

ask about family

B **DISCUSSION.**

1. How do you prefer to greet and address people?
2. How do you prefer to exchange business cards?
3. When you meet someone new, which subjects are OK to talk about?

☐ the weather ☐ your age ☐ your salary ☐ your family
☐ your job ☐ your religion ☐ your home ☐ other: _____

ED: You look familiar. Have we met before?
KEITH: I don't think so. I'm not from around here.
ED: Aren't you from Australia, or something like that?
KEITH: As a matter of fact, I am. Keith Lowe.

ED: Ed Santos. I think we met at Jack Bailey's house two weeks ago.
KEITH: Oh, that's right! Now I remember. You're Jack's colleague. What have you been up to?
ED: Not much.

D⟩ **PAIR WORK.** Discuss which of the following statements could be true, based on information in the conversation. Explain your decisions.

1. Ed and Keith are friends.
2. Ed is a businessman.
3. Keith is from another country.
4. Ed and Keith met at a party.
5. Ed and Keith both know Jack Bailey.
6. Jack Bailey is Ed's boss.

Sydney Opera House / Australia

WHAT
ABOUT **YOU?**

Which advice would you give a visitor to your country about how to behave?
Which advice do you agree with? Which do you disagree with?

It's OK to shake hands, but don't hug people!

Never ask about a person's age or salary!

Don't ask questions about a person's family.

Please don't exchange business cards with one hand!

Don't address people by their first names.

1 ▷ Get Reacquainted with Someone

🎧 CONVERSATION **MODEL** Read and listen.

A: Audrey, have you met Hanah?

B: No, I haven't.

A: Hanah, I'd like you to meet Audrey.

C: Hi, Audrey. You look familiar. I think we've met before.

B: Really? When?

C: Last month. You were at my sister Nicole's party.

B: Oh, that's right! How have you been?

🎧 Rhythm and intonation practice

 GRAMMAR. The present perfect

Use the present perfect to talk about an indefinite time in the past.
Use the simple past tense to talk about a definite time in the past.

present perfect	simple past tense
I've **met** Bill twice.	We **met** in 1999 and in 2004.
[indefinite time: We don't know when.]	[definite time: We know when.]

PAGE G1
For more …

Form the present perfect with <u>have</u> and the past participle form of a verb.

Have you **had** lunch?   Yes, I have. / No, I haven't.

Has she **seen** that new movie?   Yes, she has. / No, she hasn't.

Contractions
've eaten = have eaten
's eaten = has eaten
haven't eaten = have not eaten
hasn't eaten = has not eaten

Regular verbs
The past participle form is the same as the simple past tense form.

simple past tense	past participle
cook**ed**	cook**ed**

Irregular verbs
Look at the list of irregular verbs. For a complete list of irregular past participle forms, see Appendix, page 126.

Irregular verbs

base form	simple past tense	past participle
be	was / were	been
eat	ate	eaten
go	went	gone
have	had	had
hear	heard	heard
meet	met	met
see	saw	seen
speak	spoke	spoken
take	took	taken
write	wrote	written

 Complete each conversation with the present perfect.

1. (see)   **A:** Have you _____ that new Johnny Depp movie?   **B:** Yes, _____.

2. (visit)   **A:** Has she _____ Hong Kong?   **B:** No, _____.

3. (meet)   **A:** Have you and Mary _____ your new neighbors?   **B:** Yes, _____.

4. (write)   **A:** Has your aunt _____ any more letters?   **B:** No, _____.

5. (hear)   **A:** Have your friends _____ Sting's new CD?   **B:** Yes, _____.

Use the present perfect or the simple past tense to complete the conversations.

1. **A:** Have you seen the Taj Mahal?

   B: Yes, I have. I _____ India in 2002. The Taj Mahal _____ fantastic.
   visit   be

2. **A:** Has the new restaurant opened?

   B: No. It _____. Maybe next week.
   open / not

3. **A:** Have you eaten dinner?

   B: No, I haven't. But I _____ a big lunch only two hours ago.
   eat

4. **A:** Have they bought their tickets?

   B: I think so. They _____ to the travel agency last week.
   go

5. **A:** Have you met the new teacher?

   B: No. The class _____.
   start / not

6. **A:** Has your daughter been to Europe?

   B: Well, she _____ to the U.K. last year. But she _____
   go   be / not
   to any other countries.

CONVERSATION
PAIR WORK

Introduce classmates. If you think you've met before, get reacquainted. Or use the pictures to role-play where you may have met. Start like this:

A: _____, have you met _____?

B: _____ …

C: _____ …

in a class

at a theater

at an art exhibition

at a friend's house

at a gym

Greet a Visitor to Your Country

Sugarloaf,
Rio de Janeiro

CONVERSATION **MODEL** Read and listen.

A: Welcome to Rio. Have you ever been here before?
B: No. It's my first time. But yesterday I went to Sugarloaf. It was really beautiful.
A: That's great. Have you tried feijoada yet?
B: Feijoada? No, I haven't. What's that?
A: It's a famous Brazilian dish. I think you'll like it.

Rhythm and intonation practice

Feijoada

 A **VOCABULARY.** Tourist activities around the world. **Listen and practice.**

climb Mt. Fuji

go sightseeing
in New York

go to the top of
the Eiffel Tower

First time?
Yes.

try Korean food

And this is…

take a tour of
the Tower of London

take pictures of
the Great Wall

 B **What have <u>you</u> done?** Use the vocabulary. "I've climbed…" "I've gone sightseeing in…"

 C **GRAMMAR.** The present perfect with <u>yet</u>, <u>already</u>, <u>ever</u>, and <u>before</u>

Use <u>yet</u> at the end of questions in the present perfect to ask about recent experiences.
Have you seen the Pyramids **yet**? Has she tried Thai food **yet**?

Use <u>already</u> in affirmative statements. Use <u>yet</u> in negative statements.
I've **already** tried sushi. But I haven't tried sashimi **yet**.

Use <u>ever</u> and <u>before</u> in questions to ask about someone's life experiences.
Has Helen **ever** been to London? Has she been to London **before**?
Have you **ever** eaten feijoada? Have you **ever** eaten feijoada **before**?

GRAMMAR BOOSTER

PAGES G2–G3
For more …

D Use the words to write statements or questions in the present perfect.

1. you / go sightseeing / in London / before _____?
2. she / already / try / Guatemalan food _____.
3. they / ever / be / to Buenos Aires _____?
4. we / not take a tour of / Prague / yet _____.
5. she / go to the top of / the Empire State Building / yet _____?

E 🎧 **LISTENING COMPREHENSION.** Listen and complete the questions in the present perfect. Then listen again and check <u>yes</u> or <u>no</u> to answer each question.

	yes	no
1. Has she _____ the Great Pyramids yet?	☐	☐
2. Has he _____ in Kyoto yet?	☐	☐
3. Has she _____ ceviche yet?	☐	☐
4. Has he _____ the Pyramid of the Sun yet?	☐	☐
5. Has she _____ the Forbidden City yet?	☐	☐

The Great Pyramids / Egypt

A temple in Kyoto / Japan

ceviche / Peru

The Pyramid of the Sun / Mexico City

The Forbidden City / Beijing, China

F **PAIR WORK.** Write five questions to ask about your partner's life experiences. Write answers to your partner's questions about <u>your</u> life experiences.

| Have you ever been to Europe? | Yes, I have. I've been to Germany. |

CONVERSATION
PAIR WORK

Write a list of places to see and things to do in this city or town. Then role-play a conversation with a visitor here.

A: Welcome to _____. Have you ever been here before?
B: _____.
A: Really? Have you _____?
B: Well, _____ …

Continue the conversation in your <u>own</u> way.

Places to see:
Things to do:

CONTROLLED PRACTICE

Explain Local Customs

A READING WARM-UP. Which gestures do people use in your country?

"Come with me."

"There he is."

"Six."

B ⌒ READING. Read the article about gestures around the world. In your opinion, how are gestures different from speech?

Body Talk!

by Kelly Garbo

To communicate well with people of other countries, you must learn to speak well, right? Yes, but speaking isn't everything. Some experts say only thirty percent of communication comes from talking. Your gestures and other non-verbal actions matter, too.

But in different cultures, the same action can have different meanings. When you have to meet someone from a different culture, be prepared. Do you know what kind of gestures and customs are appropriate?

Let's look at shaking hands. North Americans like a firm handshake. But the French prefer a light, short handshake. If you shake a French person's hand the North American way, he or she may not like it. People in Eastern European countries and some Latino cultures prefer shorter handshakes, too. Hugging after shaking hands is also a common introduction there. Don't be surprised if a Brazilian gives you a hug. If you misinterpret gestures of introduction, your friendship may get off on the wrong foot!

Everyone around the world knows the "OK" hand gesture, don't they? But in Spain, parts of South America, and Eastern Europe, the OK sign is considered rude. And if you go shopping in Japan, it means you'd like your change in coins instead of bills. In France, making the OK sign means "zero" or that something is worthless. So check before you use the OK sign to be sure it's OK!

Understanding even a few key gestures from different cultures can make you a better communicator. So next time you travel, try being culturally sensitive. Find out the local gesture and let your body talk.

SOURCE: www.bellaonline.com

North Americans like a firm handshake.

C Check the statements that are true, according to Kelly Garbo. Explain why.

☐ **1.** Seventy percent of communication comes from non-verbal actions.

☐ **2.** If you don't speak someone's language, it's always safe to use gestures.

☐ **3.** French people generally don't like firm handshakes.

☐ **4.** Brazilians never shake hands.

☐ **5.** Japanese people think the OK sign is rude.

D DISCUSSION. Have you ever been surprised by someone's gestures or non-verbal actions? What was the gesture? What happened?

INTERACTION • *When in Rome . . .*

STEP 1. PAIR WORK. Read the tips about customs around the world. Discuss which ones you've never heard of before.

In the U.S.A., you should call to explain if you're going to be more than 15 minutes late for a party, lunch, or dinner.

In Taiwan, you should cover your mouth when you're using a toothpick.

In Thailand, you should never touch a person, even a child, on the head.

In Saudi Arabia, avoid asking personal questions about a person's family.

In the U.K., it is better not to ask people personal questions, about where they live, how much money they make, or what they do.

In Japan, you should take off your shoes before entering someone's home.

In Russia, wearing a coat in a public building or putting it on a chair in a restaurant is considered rude.

In Ecuador, open a gift immediately and thank the person who gave it to you.

STEP 2. GROUP WORK. Choose a topic. On your notepad, write some rules for how to behave in your country.

Topic:	
Rules:	
Are there special rules for women?	
Are there special rules for children?	

Topics
- how to meet and greet new people
- how to behave when you visit someone's home
- how to behave in a restaurant

STEP 3. DISCUSSION. Compare your notes with those of the other groups. Does everyone agree?

4 Ask about a Person's Experiences

A 🎧 **LISTENING COMPREHENSION. Listen to the game show** *Once in a Lifetime.*
Check if the contestants answered <u>yes</u> **or** <u>no</u> **to the host's questions.**

Have you ever...	Suzy		Bill	
	yes	no	yes	no
1. been to South America?	☐	☐	☐	☐
2. been to China?	☐	☐	☐	☐
3. flown in an airplane?	☐	☐	☐	☐
4. driven a bus?	☐	☐	☐	☐
5. bought a digital camera?	☐	☐	☐	☐
6. visited Chicago?	☐	☐	☐	☐

Once in a Lifetime with Pete Sosa

Have you ever...?

Pete Sosa

Suzy

Bill

B 🎧 **Now listen again and answer the questions.**

1. Where does Suzy live? Where does Bill live?
2. What does Suzy do? What does Bill do?
3. Where has Suzy been in South America?
4. Where has Suzy flown in an airplane?

C **DISCUSSION. How would** <u>you</u> **answer each of the questions from the game show?**

D 🎧 **PRONUNCIATION. Negative contractions. Notice how the /t/ sound of the
negative contraction "disappears." Listen and repeat.**

1. We haven't visited Rio.
2. He hasn't met his new boss.
3. They haven't been to Asia.
4. She hasn't eaten dinner yet.

10 UNIT 1

INTERACTION • *Getting to know you*

STEP 1. PAIR WORK. Take the survey. Check the experiences <u>you've</u> had and compare your answers with your partner's. Discuss the details of each experience.

1. Have you ever tried...?

 ☐ snake

 ☐ octopus

 ☐ guinea pig

 ☐ Swiss cheese

2. Have you ever been to...?

 ☐ Moscow

 ☐ Shanghai

 ☐ Istanbul

 ☐ Honolulu

3. Have you ever gone...?

 ☐ hang gliding

 ☐ sailing

 ☐ horseback riding

 ☐ snorkeling

How many boxes did you check?

9–12	Daredevil	Your life is just too exciting!
5–8	Go-getter	You're a real adventurer!
1–4	Fence-sitter	You're ready for more!
0	Scaredy-cat	You really should do something new!

STEP 2. WRITING. Write about an experience from the survey. Or write about what you've never done, but would like to do.

STEP 3. Walk around the room and ask your classmates questions. Complete the chart.

Find someone who has...	Name	What this person has done...
1. lived in another country.		
2. met a famous person.		
3. learned to play an instrument.		
4. eaten something unusual.		
5. done something dangerous.		

STEP 4. GROUP WORK. Choose a classmate from the chart. Introduce that person to your class.

> ❝This is Sylvia. She's learned to play two instruments: the piano and the guitar.❞

CHECKPOINT

dim sum

A 🎧 **LISTENING COMPREHENSION.** **Listen to the conversation with a tourist in Vancouver. Check <u>yes</u> or <u>no</u>.**

Has she...	yes	no
1. been to the Vancouver Aquarium yet?	☐	☐
2. been to the top of Grouse Mountain?	☐	☐
3. visited Gastown yet?	☐	☐
4. tried dim sum yet?	☐	☐
5. gone to the top of the Harbor Center Tower?	☐	☐
6. seen the Capilano Suspension Bridge yet?	☐	☐

the Vancouver Aquarium

B **Use the pictures to write questions. Don't use the same verb more than once. Use the present perfect with <u>ever</u> or <u>before</u>.**

Example: *Have you ever visited the Korean Folk Village in Yong-in, Korea* ?

1. _____ ?
2. _____ ?
3. _____ ?
4. _____ ?

The Tower of Pisa / Italy

Thai food

Mount Aconcagua / Argentina

London / U.K.

Korean Folk Village / Yong-in, Korea

C **WRITING.** **On a separate sheet of paper, write a paragraph introducing yourself to your class. Tell about some unusual experiences you've had.**

My name is Lee. I've never been to London, but...

🎵 *TOP NOTCH* SONG
"Greetings and Small Talk"
Lyrics on last book page.

TOP NOTCH PROJECT
Write a guide for a visitor to this country. Include tips to explain how to behave and how NOT to behave.

TOP NOTCH WEBSITE
For Unit 1 online activities, visit the *Top Notch* Companion Website at www.longman.com/topnotch.

Dear David,
Here I am in Europe. I've been to three countries already. I've tried

PAR AVION
030790 18H
RUE DES RENAUDES 17

David Linder
330 West Pike Street
Vancouver, B.C.
CANADA V5K 2M8

UNIT WRAP-UP

- **Social Language.** Create conversations for the tourists.

  Welcome to Paris. Have you been here before?

- **Writing.** Write a postcard from a tourist in the picture. Describe the things you have done.

UNITED KINGDOM

the Millennium Wheel

Buckingham Palace

London

A T L A N T I C   O C E A N

E U R O P E

Mozart's house

Vienna Boys' Choir

Vienna

AUSTRIA

Paris

the Eiffel Tower

crepes

FRANCE

the Campanile Tower

Venice

a gondola

ITALY

GREECE

the Parthenon

the Prado Museum

Madrid

tapas

SPAIN

moussaka

Athens

M E D I T E R R A N E A N   S E A

N
W   E
S

✔ Now I can ...

- ☐ get reacquainted with someone.
- ☐ greet a visitor to my country.
- ☐ explain local customs.
- ☐ ask about a person's experiences.

13

Movies and Entertainment

UNIT GOALS

1 Apologize for lateness
2 Discuss preferences
3 Compare tastes in movies
4 Discuss the effect of violence on viewer

 TOPIC PREVIEW. Do you rent videos or DVDs? Read the descriptions of two popular films in a movie catalog.

The Movie Lover's Catalog

If you love movies, you absolutely MUST have our catalog. It's the largest source of movies on video available in the world today. From the classics of the 30s to musicals of the Golden Age of Hollywood—and everything since—you can't beat The Movie Lover's Catalog. We have a new and expanded inventory of international films, Japanese animations, drama, comedies—even classic and current TV shows!

Frida [DVD] (2002)

Mexican painter Frida Kahlo's life is brought to the screen by director Julie Taymor and producer/star Salma Hayek. Kahlo's story is traced from her teens all the way through her complex relationship with painter husband Diego Rivera (Alfred Molina). Kahlo's search for her own identity in her paintings is covered in vivid color and with great sensitivity. Ashley Judd, Antonio Banderas, Geoffrey Rush, and Edward Norton also star.

DIRECTOR: Julie Taymor   **CATEGORY:** Drama

The Day the Earth Stood Still [VHS] (1951)

All sci-fi drama buffs will want to own this classic sci-fi drama with a message. Michael Rennie stars as Klaatu, a visitor from the stars who arrives on Earth with his robot companion, Gort. Klaatu's mission is to warn mankind about the danger of nuclear warfare. Patricia Neal, Sam Jaffe, Billy Gray also star; Robert Wise directs.

DIRECTOR: Robert Wise   **CATEGORY:** Sci-Fi & Fantasy

Also available on DVD

B DISCUSSION.

1. Where would you rather see a movie: at home or in the theater? Why?

2. Have you ever seen *Frida* or *The Day the Earth Stood Still*? Which movie would you rather rent? Explain your choice.

C 🎧 SOUND BITES. Read along silently as you listen to a natural conversation.

LISA: You're going to love this theater. You can see all the things you missed.

DAN: I'm really in the mood for a good classic movie. And on a big screen!

LISA: Much better than on the tube.

DAN: You know, I never saw *Frida*. Did you?

LISA: No. I missed it.

DAN: They say it was great. How about it?

LISA: Actually, I'd rather see something else…. Hey! They're showing *Dracula*!

DAN: Deal!

D Check the statements that are true. Explain your answers.

☐ **1.** The theater shows old movies.

☐ **2.** Dan prefers to rent a video rather than go to the movies.

☐ **3.** Lisa has already seen *Frida*.

☐ **4.** Dan's not in the mood for *Frida*.

☐ **5.** They decide to see *Dracula*.

E IN OTHER WORDS. With a partner, restate each statement in your <u>own</u> words.

1. "I'm in the mood for a good classic movie."

2. "Much better than on the tube."

3. "I missed it."

4. "Deal!"

WHAT ABOUT **YOU?**

PAIR WORK. Check the genres you like best. Then discuss movies that you've seen in each genre.

☐ comedy ☐ musical ☐ drama ☐ action ☐ science fiction ("sci-fi")

1 *Apologize for Lateness*

🎧 CONVERSATION **MODEL** **Read and listen.**

A: Sorry I'm late. Have you been here long?

B: For about 10 minutes. Not too bad.

A: I'm sorry. I got stuck in traffic.

B: The 8:00 show for *The Train* is sold out, so I got tickets for *High Flyer*. I hope that's OK.

A: That's fine. They say it's hilarious. How much do I owe?

B: Nothing. It's on me.

A: Well, thanks. Next time it's my treat.

🎧 **Rhythm and intonation practice**

Ⓐ **GRAMMAR.** **The present perfect: additional uses**

Use <u>since</u> with a time or date in the past.

> How long have you lived here? I've lived here **since 2001**.

Use <u>for</u> to describe a period of time.

> How long have you lived here? I've lived here **for five years**.

Other uses:

> with <u>always</u>: I've **always** wanted to see *Gone with the Wind*.
>
> with ordinals, the superlative, or <u>only</u>: This is **the third time** I've seen *Frida*. It's **the best** movie I've ever seen. My husband has **only** seen it once.
>
> with <u>lately</u> / <u>recently</u>, <u>just</u>: Have you seen a good movie **lately**? Yes. I've **just** seen *Seabiscuit*.
>
> with <u>still</u>, <u>so far</u>: You **still** haven't seen *Chicago*? I've seen it three times **so far**!

GRAMMAR BOOSTER

PAGES G3–G4
For more …

Ⓑ **Complete the biography of Spanish actor Antonio Banderas. Use <u>for</u> or <u>since</u>.**

Banderas has acted _____ more than 20 years. He has worked in
the theater _____ 1982, and he has acted in films _____ 1992. *The*
Mambo Kings Sing Songs of Love was his first film in English, but
Banderas didn't speak English at that time, and he had to read
his script phonetically. Banderas has had an international
reputation _____ 1988, when he appeared in *Women on the*
Verge of a Nervous Breakdown. Banderas met his wife, Melanie
Griffith, on the set of *Two Much*, and they have been married
_____ over eight years. _____ their daughter, Stella, was
born, they have lived in Los Angeles and Spain.

C PAIR WORK. **Take turns asking and answering the following questions. Use the present perfect in your answers.**

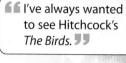
" I've always wanted to see Hitchcock's *The Birds*. "

1. Is there a movie you've always wanted to see?
2. Have you seen any good movies recently?
3. What's the best movie you've ever seen?
4. What's the worst movie you've ever seen?
5. How many movies have you seen so far this month?

D PRONUNCIATION. **Reduction of /h/. Notice how the /h/ sound "disappears." Listen and repeat.**

1. How long have you lived here?
2. Where have you worked?
3. When did he leave?
4. What's her name?

E VOCABULARY. **Some explanations for being late. Listen and practice.**

I got stuck in traffic.

I missed the bus.

I couldn't get a taxi.

I couldn't find a parking space.

F **Write two other explanations for being late.**

_____   _____

CONVERSATION PAIR WORK

Apologize for being late meeting a friend at the movies. Provide an explanation. Then, together, use the schedule to decide on a movie to see. Start like this:

A: Sorry I'm late. Have you been here long?

B: For _____ ...

War of the Planets	7:30	9:35	[7:30 sold out]
Love Me in Lima	7:45	10:20	midnight
Kitten Story	8:00	11:00	[8:00 sold out]
Better Late Than Never	7:50	10:10	

2 ▶ Discuss Preferences

MODEL **Read and listen.**

A: What would you rather see—a comedy or a musical?
B: It doesn't matter to me.
A: Well, what do you think of Madonna?
B: Actually, not much.
A: For real? She's my favorite movie star.
B: Not mine.
A: Well, that's what makes the world go 'round!

🎧 **Rhythm and intonation practice**

☹ Not much.
I don't like _____.
I can't stand _____.

☺ I love _____.
_____ 's great!

A 🎧 **VOCABULARY.** **Movie genres.** **Listen and practice.**

an action film

a horror film

a science-fiction film

an animated film

a comedy

a documentary

a drama

a musical

B **PAIR WORK.** **Compare your favorite movies for each genre.**

C 🎧 **LISTENING COMPREHENSION.** **Listen to the movie reviews and recommendations. Then use the movie genre vocabulary to complete the chart.**

Movie title	Genre	Recommended?	
		yes	no
Hot Dog			
First Things First			
Aqua-technia			
The Wolf Children			

D **DISCUSSION.** **Which movies sound good to you?** **Listen again if necessary.** **Explain.**

E ▶ GRAMMAR. Would rather

State preferences with would rather / would rather not and the base form of a verb.

I'd **rather rent** a movie than go to the theater.
He'd **rather not see** a comedy tonight.

Questions

Would you **rather** see *Star Wars* or *Frida*?
Which **would** they **rather** see—a comedy or a drama?
Would you like to rent a movie? Actually, we'd **rather not**. We're too busy.

I'd rather = I would rather

F ▶ Complete each conversation with would rather or would rather not.

1. "I'd love to see a good movie tonight."

   (YOU) Actually, _I'd rather stay home_ .

2. "I'm in the mood for a horror film."

   (YOU) Actually, _____ .

3. "Why don't we get tickets for the late show?"

   (YOU) Actually, _____ .

4. "Ben told me you wanted to rent a movie."

   (YOU) Actually, _____ .

5. "Would you like to see a comedy?"

   (YOU) Actually, _____ .

6. "How about some Italian food after the movie?"

   (YOU) Actually, _____ .

CONVERSATION PAIR WORK

Make a list of your favorite movies and movie stars. Then choose a movie to see. Use the guide, or create a new conversation.

A: What would you rather see: _____ or _____?
B: It doesn't matter to me.
A: Well, what do you think of _____?
B: Actually, _____.
A: _____ …

Continue the conversation in your own way.

My favorite movies:

My favorite movie stars:

Compare Tastes in Movies

A 🎧 **VOCABULARY. Adjectives to describe movies. Listen and practice.**

funny: something that makes you laugh

romantic: about love

boring: not interesting

weird: very strange or unusual, in a negative way

violent: containing a lot of fighting and killing

unforgettable: something that you will always remember

silly: not serious; almost stupid

B **PAIR WORK. Write a movie you know for each adjective. Compare your choices.**

a funny movie:	a violent movie:
a romantic movie:	an unforgettable movie:
a boring movie:	a silly movie:
a weird movie:	

C 🎧 **LISTENING COMPREHENSION. Listen carefully to a conversation between two people reading movie reviews from the newspaper. Choose the adjective from the vocabulary that best represents their opinions.**

romantic

D 🎧 **Listen again. Which movies do they like? Which movies do they think are bad?**

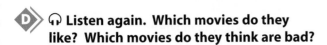

STEP 1. PAIR WORK. Read the capsule movie reviews of four classic movies. Use <u>would rather</u> to talk about which movie you'd like to see. Explain why.

BEND IT LIKE BECKHAM

⭐⭐⭐ **1/2** (PG-13, 112 minutes). An Indian girl (Parminder K. Nagra) living in London wants to play pro soccer, but her traditional Sikh parents want her to marry a nice Indian boy. Just about the perfect teenage coming-of-age comedy.

Finding Nemo

⭐⭐⭐⭐ (G, 101 minutes). A little clown fish gets lost, and his dad and another fish team up to find him. Visually beautiful, an adventure for kids plus a humorous level adults will appreciate.

The Heart of Me

⭐⭐⭐ (R, 96 minutes). Helena Bonham Carter stars as a woman who has the misfortune to fall in love with the husband (Paul Bettany) of her sister (Olivia Williams). Portrays London society, circa 1940.

Spellbound

⭐⭐⭐ (Unrated, suitable for all, 95 minutes). This Oscar-nominated U.S. documentary visits the homes of eight finalists for the National Spelling Bee, and then follows them to the finals in Washington. We get to know the kids and their families.

Source: Roger Ebert's One-Minute Reviews in the *Chicago Sun-Times*

STEP 2. On your notepad, make notes about two movies you've seen recently.

Title:	
Genre:	
Stars:	
What is the movie about?	
Adjectives:	

Title:	
Genre:	
Stars:	
What is the movie about?	
Adjectives:	

STEP 3. DISCUSSION. Talk about movies you've seen recently.

"Was it good?" "Do you recommend it?"

"Who was in it?"

"What kind of movie was it?" "What was it about?"

4 ► *Discuss the Effect of Violence on Viewers*

A ► **READING WARM-UP.** Are violent movies good entertainment, or can they be dangerous?

B ► 🎧 **READING.** Read the article about violence in movies. Which opinions do you agree with?

Can Violent Movies Be Dangerous?

Before the 1960s, most movies did not show much graphic violence. When fighting or shooting occurred on the screen, it was clean: Bang! You're dead! The victim fell to the ground and died, perhaps after speaking a few final words. The viewer never saw blood or suffering. But in the late '60s, filmmakers Arthur Penn and Sam Peckinpah began making movies with more graphic violence, such as *Bonnie and Clyde* and *The Wild Bunch*. They believed that if audiences could see how truly horrible real violence was, people would be less violent in their own lives.

Today, special effects technology has made it possible to create very realistic images of bloodshed and violence. Steven Prince, author of *Savage Cinema: Sam Peckinpah and the Rise of Ultraviolent Movies,* describes the difference between early movies and the movies of today "…filmmakers can create any image that they can dream up." So, Prince believes, because of the technology, movies today have become more and more violent and bloody.

Some people are worried that viewing a lot of violence in movies and video games can be dangerous. They feel that it can make violence seem normal and can cause people to imitate the violent behavior, to do the same thing themselves. Other people disagree. They believe that showing violence is honest and can even be helpful.

One popular filmmaker asks why violent images on the screen

Bonnie & Clyde

are a problem since we live in such a violent world. "Just open any newspaper," he says. "Any newspaper is much more violent. And those are true stories about what happens in real life. Or open any history book and read about what happens when a people are conquered."

"There's so much violence right now," says a well-known European actress. "And maybe this is the way that filmmakers speak against violence: by making violent movies."

The Wild Bunch

C ► **Check the statements that are true, according to the article.**

☐ **1.** Movies have always been very violent.
☐ **2.** Graphic violence has been common since *Bonnie and Clyde* and *The Wild Bunch*.
☐ **3.** Peckinpah and Penn thought that violence on the screen can never be good.
☐ **4.** Peckinpah and Penn thought that violent movies would make people behave more violently in their own lives.
☐ **5.** Everyone agrees that graphic violence on the movie screen is OK.

D ► **PAIR WORK.** With a partner, find a statement in the article to support each of your answers in Exercise C.

STEP 1. Complete the chart with films and television shows you know. Rate the level of violence from 0 to 3, with 3 being the most violent.

TITLE	MEDIUM	LEVEL OF VIOLENCE
Bonnie and Clyde	film	2

0 = not violent   1 = somewhat violent
2 = violent   3 = ultra violent

STEP 2. PAIR WORK. On your notepad, make notes about the most violent film or show on your chart. Tell your partner about it.

Title:	
What's it about?	
Is it dangerous for some viewers?	
Why? Why not?	

STEP 3. DISCUSSION.

1. Have movies become more violent in your lifetime? What are some examples of very violent movies?

2. Do people imitate the behavior they see in the movies? Can movies make people violent? Who should not see violent movies?

3. Can violence in other media, such as books and newspapers, also be dangerous?

> **I think** *Bonnie and Clyde* is dangerous **because** when some people see it, it's possible that they will rob banks too.

> **I disagree.** Movies are not dangerous.

> **I feel** some movies are too dangerous for children.

> **I agree.** Children imitate everything.

STEP 4. WRITING. Write a short article expressing your opinion about violence in movies and on TV.

FREE PRACTICE

CHECKPOINT

A 🎧 **LISTENING COMPREHENSION.** Listen carefully to the conversations about movies. Decide which adjective best represents each speaker's opinion.

unforgettable
boring
silly
weird
funny
romantic
violent

1. *Mediterranean Moon* is _____.
2. *The Violinist* was _____.
3. *The Good Catch* was _____.
4. *My Neighbors on Neptune* is _____.
5. *Plants of the Kalahari* is _____.
6. *Animal Opera* is _____.
7. *Crazy Horse* was _____.

B Read the DVD box labels. Then write the genre of each movie.

1. _____
2. _____
3. _____
4. _____

C Write your own response to each statement or question.

1. "Sorry I'm late."
   (YOU) _____.

2. "How long have you been here?"
   (YOU) _____.

3. "I rented *Murder at Midnight*. I hope that's OK."
   (YOU) _____.

4. "You bought the tickets? How much do I owe?"
   (YOU) _____.

5. "Next time it's my treat."
   (YOU) _____.

D Complete each statement or question with <u>for</u> or <u>since</u>.

1. That film has played at the Metroplex _____ two weeks.
2. *The Talking Parrot* has been available on DVD _____ last Tuesday.
3. I've loved the movies _____ I was a child.
4. Have you been here _____ more than an hour?

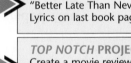

🎧 *TOP NOTCH* SONG
"Better Late Than Never"
Lyrics on last book page.

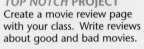

TOP NOTCH PROJECT
Create a movie review page with your class. Write reviews about good and bad movies.

TOP NOTCH WEBSITE
For Unit 2 online activities, visit the *Top Notch* Companion Website at www.longman.com/topnotch.

ult of Blood   Love in Paradise   Ticket to the Moon

:20 9:00 midnight   7:15 9:45   8:00 10:00
(sold out)

UNIT WRAP-UP

- **Social language.** Create conversations for the people.

  A: How long have you been here?
  B: About 20 minutes.

- **Writing.** Write about the picture.

  A man and woman are looking at the movie posters...

Ticket to the Moon

Love in Paradise

Cult of Blood

7:30

✓ *Now I can ...*

☐ apologize for lateness.
☐ discuss preferences.
☐ compare tastes in movies.
☐ discuss the effect of violence on viewers.

25

Staying at Hotels

UNIT GOALS
1 Leave and take a message
2 Check in
3 Request housekeeping services
4 Choose a hotel

A **TOPIC PREVIEW.** Look at the hotel bill. How many nights did the guest stay at the hotel?

Hotel del Mundo
Paseo de la Castellana 112, Madrid, Spain

Ms. Soo-Jin Hong
Paradise Apt. #105-511
Myungil-dong, Gangdong-gu
Seoul, Korea 134-756

ROOM	1102	
ARRIVAL	19/01/06	
DEPARTURE	25/01/06	
TIME	15:52	

DATE	REFERENCE	DESCRIPTION	AMOUNT
19/01	09562	Limousine	19.00
19/01	00:06:22	Overseas Call #1102	2.50
19/01		Room #1102	75.00
19/01	00:00:10	Local Call #1102	.25
20/01		Coffee Shop	7.90
20/01		Internet access 15 mins.	3.00
20/01	130354	Internet access 15 mins.	3.00
20/01	130356	Room #1102	75.00
20/01	130356	Photocopies	47.63
21/01		Minibar #1102	2.85
21/01		Coffee Shop	5.50
21/01	00:00:08	Local Call #1102	.25
21/01		Room #1102	75.00
21/01	00:00:04	Local Call #1102	.25
22/01	00:31:10	Overseas Call #1102	12.90
22/01		Room #1102	75.00
22/01		Minibar #1102	5.00
23/01		Coffee Shop	6.94
23/01	00:30:40	Overseas Call #1102	12.50
23/01		Room #1102	75.00
23/01		Minibar #1102	1.00
24/01		Room #1102	75.00
24/01		Coffee Shop	5.10
25/01	09563	Limousine	19.00
		BALANCE	604.57 (Euro)

TOTAL INCLUDING VAT*   645.46 (Euro)

GUEST SIGNATURE _____ *Soo-Jin Hong* _____

*VAT=Value Added Tax

1. INSERT CARD FIRMLY
2. PUSH DOWN HANDLE
3. OPEN DOOR
4. REMOVE CARD

Hotel del Mundo
Paseo de la Castellana 112, Madrid, Spain
1102

B **DISCUSSION.**

1. How much did the guest pay in Euros for the total bill, including tax?
2. How many phone calls did the guest make? How many times did the guest use the Internet?
3. What other services did the guest use?

C **OPTION:** Check the newspaper or the Internet to convert Euros to your local currency.

D 🎧 **SOUND BITES.** **Read along silently as you listen to a conversation in a hotel in Spain.**

GUEST: Good morning. I'm checking out. Here's my key card.
CLERK: Was your stay satisfactory?
GUEST: Yes. Very nice, thanks.
CLERK: Did you have anything from the minibar last night?
GUEST: Yes. Two bottles of spring water.

CLERK: And will you be putting this on your Vista card?
GUEST: Yes, I will.
CLERK: Here you go, ma'am. Thank you for staying with us. Will you need a taxi?
GUEST: Yes, please.

E **Check the statements that are true. Explain your answers.**

☐ **1.** The guest is leaving the hotel.
☐ **2.** The guest asks for spring water.
☐ **3.** The guest pays cash.
☐ **4.** The guest is going to the airport.

WHAT ABOUT **YOU?**

Which hotel services would you use?

 ☐ room service

 ☐ laundry

 It's 6:00 a.m. ☐ wake-up service

 ☐ minibar

 ☐ shoe shine

 ☐ babysitting

 ☐ Internet connection

 ☐ airport shuttle

 ☐ bell service

 ☐ photocopying

☐ other _____

Leave and Take a Message

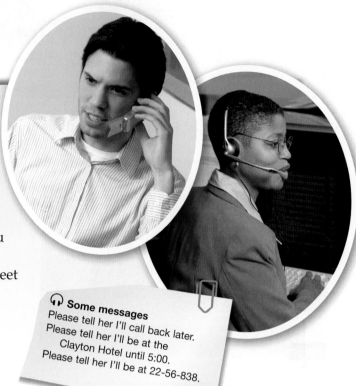

🎧 CONVERSATION **MODEL** **Read and listen.**

A: Hello? I'd like to speak to Anne Smith. She's a guest.

B: I'll ring that room for you.

• • •

B: I'm sorry. She's not answering. Would you like to leave a message?

A: Yes. Please tell her Tim Klein called. I'll meet her at the hotel at three this afternoon.

B: Is that all?

A: Yes, thanks.

🎧 **Rhythm and intonation practice**

🎧 **Some messages**
Please tell her I'll call back later.
Please tell her I'll be at the Clayton Hotel until 5:00.
Please tell her I'll be at 22-56-838.

A **GRAMMAR.** **The future with** <u>will</u>

Use <u>will</u> **and the base form of a verb to talk about the future.**

She'**ll be** back in an hour.   OK. I'**ll call** her later.

Negative statements

I **won't call** before noon.

Questions

Will you **come** at 6:00?   Yes, I will. / No, I won't.

When **will** Gary **arrive**?   At 10:00.

Remember: You can also talk about the future with <u>be going to</u>, the present continuous, or the simple present tense.

I'**m going to** leave a message.

We'**re meeting** at 3:00.

They **arrive** tomorrow.

I'll = I will
I won't = I will not

GRAMMAR BOOSTER

PAGE G5
For more ...

B **Rewrite the following future statements and questions, using** <u>will</u>**.**

1. I'm going to call her later today. _____*I'll call her later today*_____.

2. She's going to stop at the front desk first. _____.

3. My uncle is meeting my father at the airport. _____.

4. What time does the tour group get back? _____?

5. When are they going to make a reservation? _____?

6. Where is your grandmother staying in Madrid? _____?

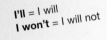

28 UNIT 3

⌐ **LISTENING COMPREHENSION.** Listen to the phone messages. Complete each message slip, according to the information you hear.

IMPORTANT MESSAGE

FOR: _____ Judy Diller _____

☑ Mr. / ☐ Ms. / ☐ Mrs. / ☐ Miss _____ Marc Pearl _____

Phone number: _____

☐ Telephoned   ☐ Please call
☐ Came to see you   ☐ Will call again
☐ Wants to see you   ☐ Returned your call

Message: _____
_____
_____

☎ **PHONE MESSAGE**

FOR: _____ Hank Pitt _____

☐ Mr. / ☑ Ms. / ☐ Mrs. / ☐ Miss _____

Phone: _____

☐ Please call   ☐ Will call again
☐ Wants to see you   ☐ Returned your call

Message: _____
_____
_____

A Message For You

FOR: _____ Collin Mack _____

☐ Mr. / ☑ Ms. / ☐ Mrs. / ☐ Miss _____

Phone: _____

☐ Called   ☐ Please call back
☐ Came to see you   ☐ Will call back
☐ Wants to meet   ☐ Returned your call

Message: _____
_____
_____

WHILE YOU WERE OUT...

FOR: _____ Patricia Carlton _____

☑ Mr. / ☐ Ms. / ☐ Mrs. / ☐ Miss _____ called.

Phone: _____

☐ Please call back
☐ Will call again

Message: _____
_____
_____

D ⌐ **PRONUNCIATION.** Contractions with <u>will</u>. **Notice that each contraction is one syllable. Listen and repeat.**

1. I'll call back later.
2. She'll be at the Clayton Hotel.
3. He'll use his credit card.
4. We'll need a limousine.
5. You'll get the bill in the mail.
6. They'll meet you at 6:00.

CONVERSATION
PAIR WORK

Role-play a phone call. Take a message on the message pad.

A: Hello? I'd like to speak to _____.
B: I'm sorry. _____. Would you like to leave a message?
A: Yes. _____ ...

Continue the conversation in your <u>own</u> way.

WHILE YOU WERE OUT ...

FOR: _____

☐ Mr. / ☐ Ms. / ☐ Mrs. / ☐ Miss _____ called.

Phone: _____

☐ Please call back
☐ Will call again

Message: _____
_____
_____

Check in

🎧 CONVERSATION
MODEL Read and listen.

A: Hi. I'm checking in. The name's Baker.
B: Let's see. That's one double for two nights. Non-smoking?
A: That's right.
B: How do you want to pay?
A: Here's my card. By the way, is the restaurant still open?
B: Actually, you'd better hurry. It closes at 9:00.

🎧 **Rhythm and intonation practice**

A 🎧 **VOCABULARY. Hotel room features.**
Listen and practice.

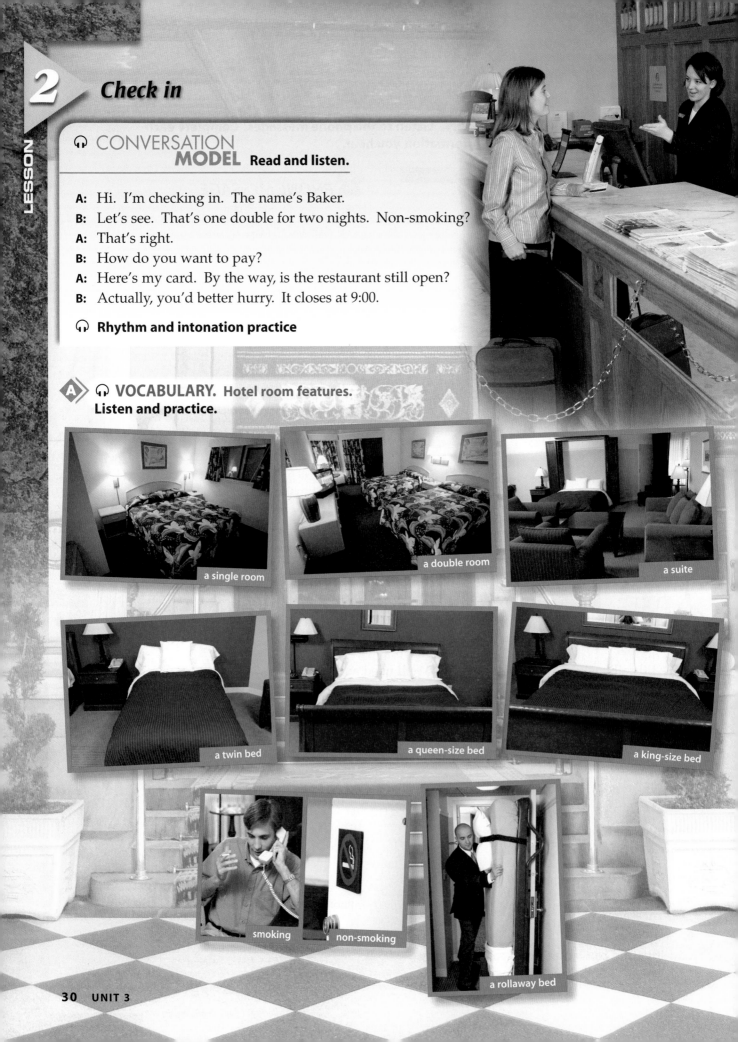

a single room

a double room

a suite

a twin bed

a queen-size bed

a king-size bed

smoking   non-smoking

a rollaway bed

B 🎧 **LISTENING COMPREHENSION.** Listen carefully to the conversations. Write the hotel room features the guest needs. Listen again and check your answers.

1. _____   2. _____   3. _____   4. _____
_____   _____   _____   _____
_____   _____   _____   _____

C **GRAMMAR.** Had better

Use **had better** to warn someone about a possible negative result.

You'**d better hurry**! You'll be late.

She'**d better make** a reservation soon. That hotel is very popular.

Negative statements

We'**d better not be** late.

Note: The contraction **'d better** is almost always used in spoken English.

GRAMMAR BOOSTER

PAGES G6–G7
For more …

D Complete each conversation with **had better** or **had better not**. Use contractions.

1. **A:** Is the museum very far from here?

   B: Yes, it is. You _____ take a taxi.

2. **A:** When does the meeting begin?

   B: Two o'clock sharp. We _____ be late.

3. **A:** It looks like rain.

   B: Well, you _____ walk. Take the bus instead.

4. **A:** It's already 9:30! I'm starving.

   B: Well, the restaurant closes at 10:30. We _____ hurry.

CONVERSATION PAIR WORK

Role-play checking in. Discuss the room features you want. Ask about the hotel facilities in the pictures.

A: Hi. I'm checking in. The name's _____.

B: _____ …

Continue the conversation in your own way.

business center

HOURS
9 a.m. to 5 p.m.

pool

HOURS
6 a.m. to 10 p.m.

gift shop

HOURS
8:00 to 21:00

fitness center

HOURS
6 a.m. to 9 p.m.

sauna

HOURS
11 a.m. to 8 p.m.

31

CONTROLLED PRACTICE

3 ▶ Request Housekeeping Services

A 🎧 **VOCABULARY.** Hotel room amenities and services. **Listen and practice.**

We need …

extra towels.

extra hangers.

skirt hangers.

an iron.

a hair dryer.

Could someone …

make up the room?

turn down the beds?

pick up the laundry?

bring up a newspaper?

take away the dishes?

B 🎧 **LISTENING COMPREHENSION.** Listen to the two phone conversations with the hotel staff. Then listen again and check the hotel services or items each guest is requesting.

Room 586		
☐ turn down the beds	☐ take away the dishes	☐ bring extra hangers
☐ bring an iron	☐ pick up the laundry	☐ bring a hair dryer
☐ bring extra towels	☐ bring skirt hangers	☐ make up the room

Room 587		
☐ turn down the beds	☐ take away the dishes	☐ bring extra hangers
☐ bring an iron	☐ pick up the laundry	☐ bring a hair dryer
☐ bring extra towels	☐ bring skirt hangers	☐ make up the room

STEP 1. PAIR WORK. Choose a guest. Tell your partner what the guest is saying.

STEP 2. Role-play telephone conversations between one of the guests and a hotel front desk clerk. Use the pictures or other ideas.

NEED HELP?

Here's language you already know:

Hotel Guest	Front Desk Clerk
We need ____.	Can I help you?
Could someone ____?	What's the problem?
Is the ____ still open?	I'm sorry to hear that.
What time does the ____ close?	How is / was the ____?
I'd like ____.	Let me check.
I'd like to ____.	Certainly.
That would be great.	You'd better hurry.

4 Choose a Hotel

A **READING WARM-UP.** What is the most important factor for you in choosing a hotel—price, location, etc.?

B 🎧 **READING.** Read the hotel guide for New York City. Which hotel sounds attractive to you?

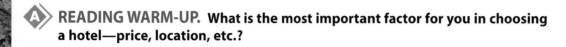

New York City has some of the best hotels in the world—and, believe it or not, some are not too expensive. But here are our picks for "the best of the best."

$$$$	Very expensive
$$$	Expensive
$$	Moderately priced
$	Budget

Most famous hotel
The Plaza Hotel $$$
768 Fifth Ave. (at 59th St.)
800 441-1414
805 rooms

Located at the southeast corner of New York's fabulous Central Park, The Plaza is as near as it gets to the best shopping along New York's famous Fifth Avenue. This 1907 hotel, with its beautiful fountain, is a famous location in many popular movies and books. Movie stars and the rich love to get married there.
4 restaurants, excellent full-service spa and health club, concierge and ticket desk, car-rental desk, business center, 24-hour room service, babysitting, laundry

SOURCE: Adapted from *Frommer's New York City 2003*

Best service at a low price
The Broadway Inn $$
264 W. 46th St. (at Eighth Ave.)
800 826-6300
41 rooms
Impeccably clean and very comfortable, this hotel is a real winner. Suites can be a great deal—with sofa, microwave, mini-fridge and lots of closet space. Located right in the noisy Theater District, the hotel is peaceful and quiet inside. Best of all are the attentive staff who work hard to make their guests happy. There is a special phone number in case guests have questions while they're out sightseeing. Note: This four-story hotel has no elevators.
2 restaurants next door, concierge, fax and copy service

Most interesting hotel
Hotel Chelsea $$
222 W. 23rd St. (between Seventh and Eighth Aves.) 212 243-3700
400 rooms, 100 available to travelers

If you're looking for the usual hotel comforts, go elsewhere. But if you're looking for atmosphere—the New York of artists, actors, and writers—this is the only place to stay. Well-known novels and plays were written here. And artists and writers live here even today. This 1884 Victorian hotel has beautiful cast-iron balconies and a busy lobby filled with artwork. Rooms are simple, but generally large. Everything is clean, but don't expect new. Not all rooms have air-conditioning. There's no room service, but the staff will be happy to help you order from local restaurants or take your clothes to the cleaners.
Restaurant, bell service, lounge

Best health club
The Peninsula-New York $$$$
700 Fifth Ave. (at 55th St.)
800 262-9467
241 rooms

The Peninsula Hotel is a place to see. Every room is high-tech with remote controls for lighting, music, TV, and air-conditioning—even in the bathroom! As a matter of fact, the huge marble bathrooms may be the most beautiful in New York City. Wonderful food service and a very helpful concierge desk ("We'll do anything guests ask, as long as it's legal."), and one of the biggest and best spa and health clubs on the roof, make this quite a hotel.
Valet parking, 2 restaurants, lounge, tri-level rooftop health club and spa with heated pool, exercise classes, whirlpool, sauna, and sundeck, 24-hour concierge, business center, 24-hour room service, in-room massage, babysitting, laundry service

For the budget-minded

The Habitat Hotel $
130 E. 57th St. (at Lexington Ave.)
Built in 1999, offers inexpensive—but small—
rooms with style. Near shopping.

The Hotel Newton $
2528 Broadway (between 94th and 95th Sts.)
A nice inexpensive hotel. Large rooms, firm beds,
and very clean.

The Lucerne $$
201 W. 79th St. (at Amsterdam Ave.)
Want comfort and service without paying high
prices? Large rooms. Great for kids.

Casablanca Hotel $$
147 W. 43rd St.
Free breakfast, coffee, tea, and cookies all day.
Free passes to a nearby health club. Small rooms.
Unusual Moroccan theme.

 PAIR WORK. Use the hotel listings to complete each statement. Explain your answers.

1. Stella Meyer is 70 years old. She likes to travel, but she has some difficulty with stairs.

   She'd better not stay at _____
   _____ .

2. Carl Ryan loves to see plays and musicals.

   He should stay at _____
   _____ .

3. Mark and Nancy Birdsall are traveling with their kids.

   They'd better stay at _____
   _____ .

4. Lucy Lee loves a hotel that is very comfortable.

   She'd better not stay at _____
   _____ .

5. Burt and Susan Rey are very active. They run and exercise every day.

   They should stay at _____
   _____ .

TOP NOTCH
INTERACTION

The best of the best!

STEP 1. How important are these factors for you in choosing a hotel? Rate these on a scale of 1 to 5. Compare your answers with a partner's.

	not important	very important

price	1 - 2 - 3 - 4 - 5
room size	1 - 2 - 3 - 4 - 5
cleanliness	1 - 2 - 3 - 4 - 5
location	1 - 2 - 3 - 4 - 5
service	1 - 2 - 3 - 4 - 5
amenities	1 - 2 - 3 - 4 - 5
atmosphere	1 - 2 - 3 - 4 - 5

STEP 2. PAIR WORK. Look at all the hotel listings and the map of New York. Choose a hotel. Discuss the advantages and disadvantages of the hotels.

STEP 3. Tell your class about the hotel you chose.

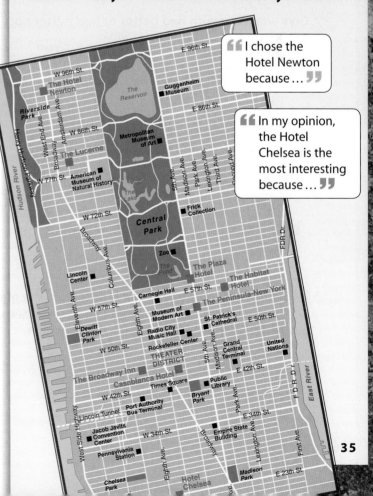

"I chose the Hotel Newton because…"

"In my opinion, the Hotel Chelsea is the most interesting because…"

A 🎧 **LISTENING COMPREHENSION.** **Listen carefully to the conversations. Then listen again and check the hotel service or services each person needs.**

	room service	laundry service	shoe shine service	wake-up service	extra hangers	extra towels	make up room
1.	☐	☐	☐	☐	☐	☐	☐
2.	☐	☐	☐	☐	☐	☐	☐
3.	☐	☐	☐	☐	☐	☐	☐
4.	☐	☐	☐	☐	☐	☐	☐

B **What hotel room feature should each guest ask for? Explain your answers.**

1. Ms. Gladstone is traveling alone. She doesn't need much space. _a single room_

2. Mr. and Mrs. Moore are checking into a single room. Their twelve-year-old daughter is with them. _____

3. Donald Lattanzio is very big and tall. He needs a good night's sleep for an important meeting tomorrow. _____

4. Nicole Miller plans to have several meetings with her colleagues. She'd rather not leave the hotel. _____

5. Paul Preston's company wants him to save some money by sharing a room with a colleague. _____

C **Give warnings with __had better__ or __had better not__. Use contractions.**

1. "It's raining. I'm going outside." **YOU** _You'd better take an umbrella_.

2. "It takes Janet 30 minutes to walk to school. Class begins in 15 minutes."
   YOU _____.

3. "My father is arriving at the airport at 6:00. It's almost 5:30 now."
   YOU _____.

4. "We're having an English test tomorrow."
   YOU _____.

5. "I haven't had a vacation in two years."
   YOU _____.

D **WRITING. Choose one of the hotels from the guide on pages 34–35 and write why you would like to stay there. Or write real information about a hotel you have stayed at.**

> Last summer my family and I stayed in a little
> hotel at the beach. The hotel was near the ...

TOP NOTCH PROJECT
Where would you like to go for vacation? Use the Internet or a travel guide to find a hotel there. Write the advantages and disadvantages of the hotel.

TOP NOTCH WEBSITE
For Unit 3 online activities, visit the *Top Notch* Companion Website at www.longman.com/topnotch.

UNIT WRAP-UP

- **Social language.** Create conversations for the people.
- **Grammar.** Ask questions with <u>will</u> about the picture. Answer the questions.
- **Writing.** Write a description about the hotel for a hotel guide book.

ROOM 816

BELL DESK

RECEPTION

THE BELMAR HOTEL

DIRECTORY

BUSINESS CENTER
9:00 A.M. – 4:00 P.M.   2

GIFT SHOP
9:00 A.M. – 9:00 P.M.   Lobby

FITNESS CENTER
6:00 A.M. – 10:00 P.M.   3

SPA
10:00 A.M. – 3:00 P.M.   5

SKYTOP RESTAURANT
8:00 A.M. – 11:00 P.M.   12

✔ *Now I can ...*

☐ leave and take messages.
☐ check in.
☐ request housekeeping services.
☐ choose a hotel.

37

Cars and Driving

UNIT GOALS

1 Describe an accident
2 Get service at a service station
3 Rent a car
4 Understand international driving rules

A TOPIC PREVIEW. Read the e-mail. Explain what it's for.

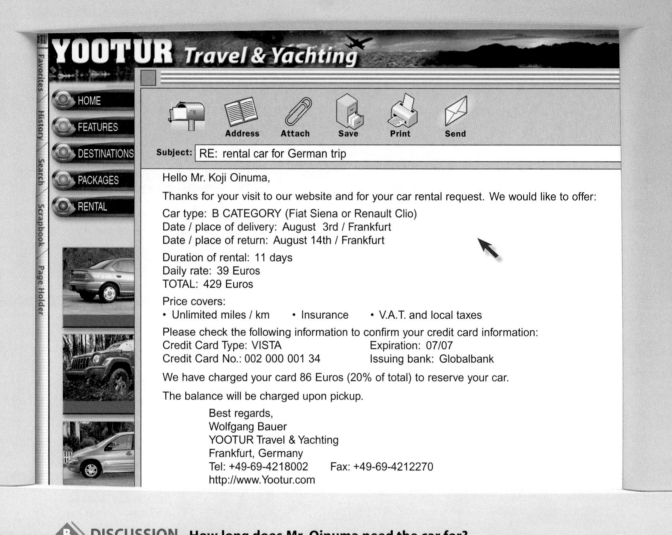

YOOTUR *Travel & Yachting*

Favorites | History | Search | Scrapbook | Page Holder

- HOME
- FEATURES
- DESTINATIONS
- PACKAGES
- RENTAL

Address Attach Save Print Send

Subject: RE: rental car for German trip

Hello Mr. Koji Oinuma,

Thanks for your visit to our website and for your car rental request. We would like to offer:

Car type: B CATEGORY (Fiat Siena or Renault Clio)
Date / place of delivery: August 3rd / Frankfurt
Date / place of return: August 14th / Frankfurt

Duration of rental: 11 days
Daily rate: 39 Euros
TOTAL: 429 Euros

Price covers:
- Unlimited miles / km   • Insurance   • V.A.T. and local taxes

Please check the following information to confirm your credit card information:
Credit Card Type: VISTA   Expiration: 07/07
Credit Card No.: 002 000 001 34   Issuing bank: Globalbank

We have charged your card 86 Euros (20% of total) to reserve your car.

The balance will be charged upon pickup.

　　　　Best regards,
　　　　Wolfgang Bauer
　　　　YOOTUR Travel & Yachting
　　　　Frankfurt, Germany
　　　　Tel: +49-69-4218002   Fax: +49-69-4212270
　　　　http://www.Yootur.com

B DISCUSSION. How long does Mr. Oinuma need the car for? How much will it cost per day? How much does he pay for the reservation?

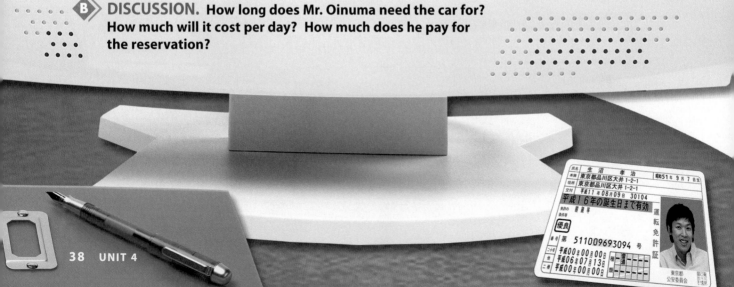

C ⌒ **SOUND BITES.** Read along silently as you listen to a conversation in a car rental agency in Germany.

RENTER: Good morning. Koji Oinuma. I have a reservation.

AGENT: Certainly, sir. Just a moment … Oh, yes. We were expecting you. An air-conditioned Clio. Is that with automatic transmission, or manual?

RENTER: Either way.

AGENT: I'll need to see your driver's license and a major credit card.

RENTER: Here you go.

AGENT: I have you returning the car on August 14?

RENTER: That's correct.

AGENT: And will that be here at the airport?

RENTER: Yes. At about 4 p.m. Is that OK?

AGENT: That'll be fine. Here are the keys. The car's right outside.

D Read the conversation again. Check the statements that are true. Explain each response.

- ☐ **1.** The car rental agent knew Mr. Oinuma was coming for a car.
- ☐ **2.** Mr. Oinuma needs to show the agent his passport.
- ☐ **3.** The conversation is in an airport.
- ☐ **4.** Mr. Oinuma will return the car on August 14 in the morning.
- ☐ **5.** Mr. Oinuma pays for the car rental with a credit card.

WHAT ABOUT **YOU?**

Choose a place you'd like to go, a travel date, and a car you'd like to rent. Fill out the online rental request for yourself.

PAIR WORK. Tell your partner where you're going. Did you select the same car?

Sunshine Rentals

Rent-a-Car Booking / Request

Pickup City or Airport:

Return City or Airport:

Car Type:

Pickup Date: (D/M/Y)

Return Date: (D/M/Y)

SEARCH NOW

1 *Describe an Accident*

CONVERSATION MODEL Read and listen.

A: I had an accident.

B: I'm so sorry. Are you OK?

A: I'm fine. No one was hurt.

B: Thank goodness. How did it happen?

A: Well, the other driver was tailgating, and he hit my car.

B: Oh, no! Was there much damage?

A: No. I'll only have to replace a taillight.

Rhythm and intonation practice

Ways to show concern
Oh, no!
I'm so sorry.
How awful!
I'm sorry to hear that.

A VOCABULARY. Car parts. Listen and practice.

EXTERIOR

1. headlight
2. engine
3. hood
4. windshield wiper
5. windshield
6. window
7. trunk
8. taillight
9. signal
10. bumper
11. tire
12. door
13. side-view mirror

INTERIOR

1. steering wheel
2. horn
3. dashboard
4. gas pedal
5. clutch
6. brake pedal
7. gearshift
8. rearview mirror
9. emergency brake
10. seat belt

B GRAMMAR. The past continuous

Form the past continuous with <u>was</u> or <u>were</u> and a present participle.

What **were** you **doing** last night at eight? I **was watching** TV.

Was the car **making** that noise this morning? Yes, it was. / No, it wasn't.

**The past continuous shows an action that continued during a period of time in the past.
The simple past tense shows an action that occurred and then ended.**

past continuous   simple past tense
I **was going** too fast when I **had** the accident.

GRAMMAR BOOSTER

PAGE G7
For more ...

C Complete the paragraph with the past continuous or the simple past tense.

I _____ an accident on the way to work. I _____ slowly and
    1. have   2. drive
I thought I _____ attention. The problem was that I _____ an
         3. pay   4. wait for
important phone call. When the cell phone _____, I just _____ it.
                                               5. ring   6. answer
All of a sudden, the car in front of me _____, and I _____ it.
                                            7. stop   8. hit
I certainly _____ my lesson. Luckily, I _____ a seat belt when
              9. learn   10. wear
I _____ the accident.
     11. have

D 🎧 LISTENING COMPREHENSION. Listen and write the number of the conversation for each picture. Then listen again to check your work.

_____

_____

_____

_____

CONVERSATION
PAIR WORK

**Role-play a conversation about an accident.
Use the pictures or your <u>own</u> ideas.
Start like this:**

A: I had an accident.

B: _____. How did it happen?

A: _____.

B: Was there much damage?

A: _____.

speeding

not paying attention

tailgating

talking on a cell phone

CONTROLLED PRACTICE

2 · Get Service at a Service Station

🎧 CONVERSATION **MODEL** **Read and listen.**

A: Fill it up, please, with regular.

B: Yes, sir. Anything else?

A: My turn signal isn't working. Can you fix it?

B: Yes, we can. Can you drop the car off tomorrow morning at about 9:00?

A: Sure. What time can I pick it up?

B: How about noon?

A: Terrific. I'll see you at 9:00.

🎧 **Rhythm and intonation practice**

🎧 **Polite address**

Yes, sir.   Yes, ma'am.

A 🎧 **VOCABULARY. Some phrasal verbs. Listen and practice.**

1. turn on

2. fill up

3. pick up

4. turn off

5. drop off

B **Complete each sentence with one of the phrasal verbs.**

1. I need gas. Can you please _____?
   drop it off / fill it up

2. It's raining, and the windshield wipers are broken. I can't _____.
   turn them on / turn them off

3. The car is ready. Can you _____ today at 5:00?
   drop it off / pick it up

4. We can do the service on Tuesday. Please _____ early.
   drop it off / pick it up

5. What's wrong with these headlights? I can't _____.
   fill them up / turn them off

GRAMMAR. Direct object placement with phrasal verbs

Phrasal verbs contain a main verb and a particle (a preposition or adverb) that together have their own meaning.

main verb		particle	
turn	+	on	= start (a machine)

With certain phrasal verbs, direct object nouns can come before or after the particle.

I'll **drop off** the car. OR I'll **drop** the car **off**.

Direct object pronouns, however, must come before the particle.

I'll **drop it off**. (NOT I'll ~~drop off it.~~)

Did you **fill them up**? (NOT Did you ~~fill up them?~~)

Where will they **pick us up**? (NOT Where will they ~~pick up us?~~)

GRAMMAR BOOSTER

PAGE G8
For more ...

D 🎧 **PRONUNCIATION.** Stress of particles in phrasal verbs. **Notice the change in stress when an object pronoun comes before the particle. Listen and repeat.**

1. **A:** I'd like to drop off the car.

   B: OK. What time can you drop it off?

2. **A:** They need to pick up the keys.

   B: Great. When do they want to pick them up?

E Unscramble the words to write statements or questions. Then read the sentences aloud.

1. The taillights aren't working. (can't / I / on / them / turn) _____.

2. The car needs service. (off / drop / service station / at / the / I'll / it) _____.

3. It's too cold for air conditioning. (switch / Which / off / it / turns) _____?

4. Thanks for fixing the car. (it / pick / What time / I / can / up) _____?

5. The car is almost out of gas. (up / Please / fill / it) _____.

CONVERSATION
PAIR WORK

Practice asking for service and repairs. Review the vocabulary on page 40.

A: Fill it up, please, with regular.

B: _____. Anything else?

A: _____. Can you _____?

B: _____ ...

Continue the conversation in your <u>own</u> way.

💡 **Some ideas...**
- won't turn on / turn off
- won't open / close
- (is) making a funny sound
- (is) not working
- (is) stuck

3 Rent a Car

A ∩ VOCABULARY. Types of cars. Listen and practice.

a sedan

a station wagon

a van

a convertible

an SUV

a sports car

a luxury car

a compact car

a full-size car

B PAIR WORK. Choose the best kind of car for each person. Discuss your reasons with your partner.

 1 Mr. Taylor is a businessman from Geneva, Switzerland, attending a business meeting in Kota Kinabalu, Malaysia. He doesn't have a lot of luggage. He only needs the car for local travel.

car type: _a compact car_

reason: _He's traveling alone and doesn't_
need a large car.

2 Ms. Peres is a banker from Porto Alegre, Brazil. Her daughter is getting married in Puebla, Mexico. She wants to drive there from Mexico City with her husband and two other children for the wedding. They have a lot of clothes and presents for the wedding.

car type: _____

reason: _____

 **3** Mr. Soo is a tourist from Korea, visiting western Australia with his brother. They enjoy hiking and fishing, and they're planning a road trip through the lake district. They plan to drive on some rough roads, so they want a car with four-wheel drive.

car type: _____

reason: _____

 4 Ms. Montez is a tourist from Veracruz, Mexico, visiting national parks and cities in the U.S. with her husband and their five children. They plan to do a lot of shopping.

car type: _____

reason: _____

 5 Dr. Sato is from Osaka, Japan. He's traveling to an international medical meeting in Buenos Aires, Argentina. He has to invite three doctors to dinner and after-dinner entertainment. He likes to drive.

car type: _____

reason: _____

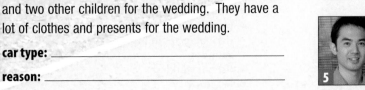

C 🎧 **LISTENING COMPREHENSION.** **Listen to the phone conversations.**
Did the caller rent the car?

If so, what kind? [or]	If not, why not?
1._____	_____
2._____	_____
3._____	_____
4._____	_____

TOP NOTCH
INTERACTION • *Let's rent a car!*

STEP 1. **On your notepad, plan a trip for which you need a rental car.**

destination	pickup date	drop-off date	number of companions	activities

STEP 2. ROLE PLAY. **Choose one or both situations for your trip:**

• A telephone call to a car rental agency. Discuss car types, explain your needs, and rent a car for your trip.

• A telephone call to a car rental agency after an accident. Report the accident. Say what you were doing when you had the accident. Discuss repairs.

NEED HELP? **Here's language you already know:**

Express concern
How did it happen?
Oh, no!
How awful!
I'm so sorry.
I'm sorry to hear that.
Thank goodness!

Offer help
How can I help you?
Certainly, sir / ma'am.
When will you drop off / pick up the car?
That'll be fine.

Describe damage
The ___ is / are broken.
The ___ is / are not working.
The ___ won't open / close / turn on / turn off.
The ___ is stuck.

Discuss the accident
Was there much damage?
I / The other driver was [speeding].
I hit another car.
Another car hit me.
No one was hurt.

Rent a car
I'd like a [compact car].
I need a car with [automatic / manual] transmission.

4

Understand International Driving Rules

A **READING WARM-UP.** Are you a good driver? If you don't drive a car, would you like to learn?

B 🎧 **READING.** Read the article about driving a car abroad. Do you think this information is important?

TIPS ON DRIVING ABROAD

It can be difficult to drive in another country. First, driving rules and laws differ from country to country. So do road signs. And, people in different countries drive on opposite sides of the road! Here are some tips on driving abroad.

First, obtain an International Driving Permit (IDP). Most countries accept this permit. It's easy to get an IDP. Just enter "International Driving Permit" in any Internet search engine and you will get the information you need.

Once you have the IDP, carry your own driver's license with you any time you drive outside your own country.

If possible, get a copy of the foreign country's rules before you begin driving in that country. An excellent source of information is a car rental company in the foreign country.

Be aware:
- Some countries have a minimum and maximum driving age.
- Some countries have penalties for drivers and/or passengers who don't wear a seat belt. Always "buckle up."
- Many countries require you to honk your horn before going around a sharp corner or to flash your lights before passing.
- If the drivers in the country you are visiting drive on the opposite side of the road from your own country, it may be a good idea to practice driving in a quiet area before attempting to drive in heavy traffic.

And a word about road signs: In general, the color red on an international road sign signals negative information, such as a warning or prohibition, whereas blue is positive. Simply put, blue says *do*, red says *don't*.

SOURCE: http://travel.state.gov

See how many international road signs you know.

2	SLIPPERY ROAD	1
	MINIMUM SPEED	
	MAXIMUM SPEED [SPEED LIMIT]	2
	NO PASSING	
	DANGER	3
	PEDESTRIAN CROSSING	
	NO ENTRY	4
	PARKING AREA	
	NO STOPPING	5
	NO PARKING	

10   9   8   7   6

Answers: 1. NO ENTRY   2. SLIPPERY ROAD   3. PEDESTRIAN CROSSING   4. DANGER   5. NO PASSING   6. NO STOPPING   7. PARKING AREA   8. MINIMUM SPEED   9. MAXIMUM SPEED   10. NO PARKING

SOURCE: http://www.ideamerge.com

C **Check all the statements that are true, according to the article. Explain your responses.**

☐ **1.** It's difficult to get an international driving permit to drive in another country.

☐ **2.** You should always carry your driver's license when you drive in another country.

☐ **3.** Foreign car rental companies can tell you local driving rules.

☐ **4.** It's never necessary to wear a seat belt outside of your own country.

☐ **5.** The color of a road sign can help you understand what it means.

D **DISCUSSION.** Discuss the difficulties of driving abroad. What should you do before the trip?

TOP NOTCH
INTERACTION • *What makes a good driver?*

STEP 1. PAIR WORK. With your partner, complete the survey about bad
driving practices. (If you don't drive, answer the questions about
someone you know.)

Do you ...

☐ speed?

☐ tailgate?

☐ honk your horn
unnecessarily?

☐ cut off other
drivers?

☐ talk on a cell phone
when you drive?

☐ not pay
attention?

☐ not stop at
stop signs?

☐ not signal?

☐ flash your lights
at other drivers?

☐ weave through
traffic?

Score one point for each check.

	POINTS	0–1	2–4	5–7	8–10
ACCIDENT PROBABILITY		ALMOST 0%			100%

STEP 2. PAIR WORK. Discuss do's and
don'ts for drivers. Make a list on
your notepad. Compare your list
with other classmates' lists.

do:	don't:
buckle up	tailgate

STEP 3. WRITING. On a separate sheet
of paper, write about good
drivers and bad drivers. Use
your notepad and the survey for
support.

Good drivers know the driving rules and laws. They always stop ...

FREE PRACTICE

47

A 🎧 **LISTENING COMPREHENSION.** Listen carefully to the people renting cars. Write the number of the conversation below the kind of car they want.

_____   _____   _____   _____   _____   _____

B **Choose a response to each statement or question.**

1. "Was there any damage?"
   a. Yes. He was tailgating.   **b.** Yes. The taillights are broken.

2. "Fill it up, please."
   a. Sure. What time can I pick it up?   **b.** Sure. Anything else?

3. "No one was hurt."
   a. I'm so sorry to hear that.   **b.** Thank goodness.

4. "I was talking on my cell phone, and I hit another car."
   a. Oh, no!   **b.** Was he speeding?

C **Complete each statement about cars.**

1. A small, fast car is a _____sports car_____.

2. When you drive too fast, you are _____.

3. The light that indicates the direction you want to turn is the _____.

4. The lights on the front of the car are the _____.

5. If you want to check the engine, you have to open the _____.

6. When you want to stop or slow the car, step on the _____.

D **Complete each statement or question with the past continuous or the simple past tense.**

1. I _____, and I _____ an accident.
   _{speed}   _{have}

2. The other driver _____ a seat belt, and
   _{not wear}
   she _____ at the stop sign.
   _{not stop}

3. She _____ on a cell phone and _____.
   _{talk}   _{not pay attention}

4. Who _____ when the accident _____?
   _{drive}   _{happen}

5. Where _____ they _____ when the
   _{go}
   phone _____?
   _{ring}

🎧 *TOP NOTCH* SONG
"Wheels Around the World"
Lyrics on last book page.

TOP NOTCH **PROJECT**
Research car accidents in your local newspaper or on the Internet. Describe an accident to your class.

TOP NOTCH **WEBSITE**
For Unit 4 online activities, visit the *Top Notch* Companion Website at www.longman.com/topnotch.

AEROPUERTO / AIRPORT TEMUCO, CHILE

UNIT WRAP-UP

- **Narration.** Tell a story, using the pictures.
- **Social language.** Create conversations for the people.
- **Writing.** Describe the accident and its causes.

MULTI CAR RENTALS

January 16

Pucon, Chile

JANUARY 16
ARRIVAL
14:45

January 17

January 18

MULTI CAR RENTALS

Later

✓ Now I can ...

- ☐ describe an accident.
- ☐ get service at a service station.
- ☐ rent a car.
- ☐ understand international driving rules.

49

Personal Care and Appearance

UNIT GOALS

1 Ask for something you can't find
2 Request salon services
3 Schedule and pay for personal care
4 Discuss ways to improve appearance

A ▷ TOPIC PREVIEW. Which of these products do you buy regularly? Where do you buy them: in a drugstore, a cosmetics store, online, or someplace else?

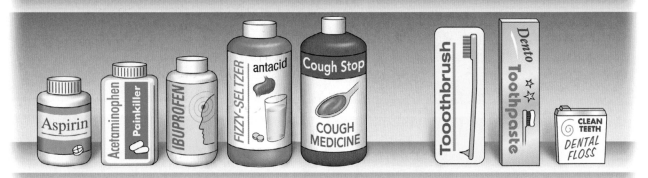

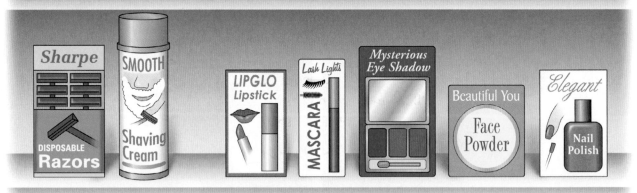

B ▷ PAIR WORK. With your partner, classify the products and write them in the chart.

Hair care	Tooth care	Skin care	Shaving	Makeup	Medicine
shampoo					

C 🎧 **SOUND BITES. Read along silently as you listen to a conversation at a meeting in Brazil.**

MIEKO: Hey, Noor. I need to pick up a few things on the way back to the hotel. Feel like stopping at a cosmetics store? We could get some of that makeup these gorgeous Brazilians wear.

NOOR: I'd like to, but I think I'll pass. I don't have much time today. I'm expecting an important call from Kuala Lumpur in a few minutes.

MIEKO: No problem. I'll just go myself. But wish me luck. I'm sure no one speaks Japanese!

NOOR: Don't worry. Most people speak some English. You'll be fine.

MIEKO: I guess. In any case, the store's self-service. It'll be a piece of cake!

NOOR: See you back at the hotel.

D Read the conversation again. Correct the following false statements.

1. Mieko is going to shop in a store in the hotel.
2. Noor can't go with Mieko because she has to call Kuala Lumpur.
3. Noor is worried that no one speaks Japanese.

E **UNDERSTANDING MEANING FROM CONTEXT. Complete each statement, according to the conversations.**

1. When Noor says, "I think I'll pass," she means _____.
2. When Noor says, "You'll be fine," she means _____.
3. When Mieko says, "It'll be a piece of cake," she means _____.

WHAT ABOUT **YOU?**

Complete the chart about the things <u>you</u> buy and your reasons.

Product	What brand?	Reason
shampoo		
soap		
toothpaste		

DISCUSSION. On the board, write a list of all the shampoo, soap, and toothpaste brands your classmates use. Do you all agree on which brands are the best?

1 Ask for Something You Can't Find

∩ CONVERSATION MODEL Read and listen.

A: Excuse me. Where would I find toothpaste?
B: Toothpaste? Have a look in aisle two.
A: Actually, I did and there wasn't any.
B: I'm sorry. Let me get you some from the back.
A: Thanks so much.

∩ **Rhythm and intonation practice**

A ∩ **VOCABULARY. Personal care products. Listen and practice.**

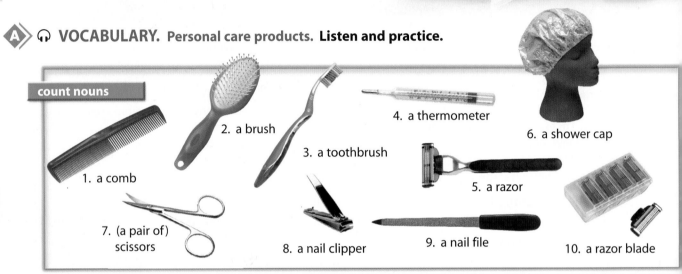

count nouns

1. a comb
2. a brush
3. a toothbrush
4. a thermometer
5. a razor
6. a shower cap
7. (a pair of) scissors
8. a nail clipper
9. a nail file
10. a razor blade

non-count nouns

1. soap
2. deodorant
3. toothpaste
4. hair spray
5. sunscreen
6. dental floss
7. makeup
8. shampoo
9. shaving cream
10. body lotion

B ∩ **LISTENING COMPREHENSION. Listen carefully to the ads for personal care products. Choose the kind of product it is. Then listen again and check your work.**

1. Spring Rain ☐ shampoo ☐ deodorant
2. Rose ☐ soap ☐ conditioner
3. Pro-Tect ☐ hand cream ☐ sunscreen
4. All Over ☐ body lotion ☐ soap
5. Scrubbie ☐ toothpaste ☐ shaving cream

C. GRAMMAR. Count and non-count nouns: indefinite quantities and amounts

Some and any

Use **some** and **any** with both count and non-count nouns.

Use some in affirmative statements.

We bought **some** nail files. Now we have **some**.

They need **some** soap. We have **some**.

Use some or any in questions.

Do you want **some** shampoo? OR Do you want **any** shampoo?

Use any in negative statements.

I don't have **any** razors, and I don't want **any**.

We don't want **any** deodorant. We don't need **any**.

A lot of, many, and much

Use **a lot of** with both count and non-count nouns in statements and questions.

That store has **a lot of** razors. They don't have **a lot of** nail files. Do they have **a lot of** lotion?

Use **many** and **much** in negative statements.

Use many with count nouns.

They don't have **many** brands of makeup.

Use much with non-count nouns.

The store doesn't have **much** toothpaste.

GRAMMAR BOOSTER

PAGES G8–G9
For more …

D. Complete the conversation between a husband and a wife getting ready for a family trip.

DANA: Do we have _____ shampoo?
<u>1. any / many</u>

NEIL: Yes. We have _____ shampoo.
<u>2. many / a lot of</u>

DANA: And Maggie uses _____ conditioner. Is there _____?
<u>3. much / a lot of</u>   <u>4. many / any</u>

NEIL: No. There isn't _____ conditioner. And we don't have _____
<u>5. some / any</u>   <u>6. much / many</u>

toothpaste, either. I can pick _____ up on my way home.
<u>7. some / any</u>

DANA: Hey, Adam's shaving now. Does he need _____ razor blades?
<u>8. any / much</u>

What about _____ aftershave lotion?
<u>9. some / many</u>

NEIL: He doesn't shave every day. He can use mine.

CONVERSATION PAIR WORK

Role-play shopping for personal care products. Use the directory.

A: Excuse me. Where would I find _____?

B: _____? Have a look in aisle _____.

A: Actually, _____.

B: _____ …

Continue the conversation. Ask about other personal care products.

Cosmetics Plus Directory	
	AISLE
Hair Care	3
Tooth Care	4
Skin Care	2
Nail Care	2
Makeup	2
Cold and Flu Medicine	1
Shaving Supplies	1

CONTROLLED PRACTICE

2 Request Salon Services

LESSON

🎧 CONVERSATION MODEL Read and listen.

A: I'm Linda Court. I have a two o'clock appointment for a haircut with Sean.

B: Hello, Ms. Court. Sean's running a little late. Can I get you some coffee or tea?

A: No, thanks. Can I get a manicure in the meantime?

B: Yes, but it'll be a few minutes. There's someone ahead of you.

🎧 **Rhythm and intonation practice**

A 🎧 VOCABULARY. Salon services. Listen and practice.

1. a shampoo

2. a shave

3. a haircut

4. a manicure

5. a pedicure

B GRAMMAR. Someone / anyone

Use **someone** in affirmative statements.
There's **someone** ahead of you.

Use **anyone** in negative statements.
There isn't **anyone** waiting.

Use **someone** or **anyone** in questions.
Can **someone** wash my hair?
Can **anyone** give me a manicure?

GRAMMAR BOOSTER
PAGE G10
For more ...

C Complete each statement or question with someone or anyone.

1. There's _____ at the front desk.
2. They didn't tell _____ that it would be a long wait.
3. Did you see _____ giving a manicure?
4. I don't have the scissors. I gave them to _____.
5. There will be _____ here to give you a pedicure in a few minutes, if you can wait.

6. Please don't tell _____ the price. It was very expensive!

7. Did you tell _____ how long you've been waiting?

8. _____ called and left you this message while you were getting your shampoo.

9. Please give this list of services to _____ to check.

10. There wasn't _____ there when she called for an appointment.

11. _____ told me to wait a few minutes.

12. I didn't ask _____ about the price.

D 🎧 **LISTENING COMPREHENSION. Listen carefully to the conversations. Check the service(s) each client wants.**

1.	☐	☐	☐	☐	☐
2.	☐	☐	☐	☐	☐
3.	☐	☐	☐	☐	☐
4.	☐	☐	☐	☐	☐

E 🎧 **PRONUNCIATION. Vowel reduction to /ə/. The vowel in an unstressed syllable is often reduced to /ə/. Listen and repeat.**

1. ma ni cure
/ə/

2. pe di cure
/ə/

3. me di cine
/ə/

4. de o do rant
/ə/

CONVERSATION
PAIR WORK

Role-play requesting salon services. Use the list. Start like this:

A: I'm _____. I have _____ appointment for a _____ with _____.

B: Hello, _____. _____'s running a little late. Can I get you some _____?

A: _____ …

Continue the role play in your own way.

UNISEX SALON
Services   Staff

shampoo   Lisa / Olga

haircut   Judy / Christopher / Bruce

manicure   Sonia / Natasha

pedicure   Karin

shave   Nick

3 ⟩ *Schedule and Pay for Personal Care*

A 🎧 **VOCABULARY.** Schedule and pay for personal care.
Listen and practice.

Would it be possible to get a facial?
I don't have an appointment.

How long will I have to wait?

How much do you charge
for a massage?

Is it customary to leave a tip?

Can I charge it to my room?

I'm sorry. I have to cancel
my appointment.

B ⟩ **Complete each conversation. Use the expressions from the vocabulary and
your <u>own</u> ideas.**

1. **A:** _____?
   B: Let me check the price list.

2. **A:** _____?
   B: Well, you're in luck. A customer just canceled his appointment.

3. **A:** _____?
   B: Certainly. What's your room number?

4. **A:** _____?
   B: About 35 minutes. Is that OK?

5. **A:** _____?
   B: Yes, it is. Most people give about 10 percent.

C 🎧 **LISTENING COMPREHENSION.** Listen to the conversations in a salon.
**Check what each client asks about. Then listen again and explain to a partner
what happened.**

1. **a.** ☐ getting a massage   **b.** ☐ getting a manicure

2. **a.** ☐ waiting for a manicure   **b.** ☐ paying for a manicure

3. **a.** ☐ getting a haircut   **b.** ☐ charging a haircut to her room

4. **a.** ☐ tipping someone   **b.** ☐ getting a shampoo

INTERACTION • *Pamper yourself!*

ROLE PLAY. Look at the date book of the Finis Terra Hotel. Role-play conversations to request services, schedule appointments, and ask about payment.

Finis Terra
HOTEL & SPA

SATURDAY, JULY 10 192/174

	Spa facial	Deluxe manicure	Full massage	Neck and shoulder massage	Pedicure and foot massage
				Kevin	May
	Katya	Lucille	Tom	Ms. Cruz	
9 00	Mr. Santos				
9 15					
9 30					Mr. Loyola
9 45					
10 00	Ms. Pleva	Mr. Drucker			
10 15					
10 30			Mr. Yu		
10 45					
11 00	Ms. Kumar				
11 15					Ms. Joon
11 30					
11 45		Ms. Gomez			
12 00					
12 15				Ms. Benson	
12 30					
12 45					
1 00	Mr. Dialo				
1 15					
1 30					
1 45					
2 00					
2 15					
2 30					

NEED HELP? Here's language you already know:

Payment
How much do you charge for a ____?
Can I charge it to my room?
Is it customary to leave a tip?

Client
Can I get a ____?
Would it be possible to get a ____?
How long will I have to wait?
Can I get a ____ in the meantime?
I'm ____. I have ____ appointment for a ____ with ____.

Salon's Staff
It'll be a few minutes.
There's someone ahead of you.
You're in luck.
[She's] running a little late.
Can I get you [some tea]?

JULY 11 193/173

4 *Discuss Ways to Improve Appearance*

A **READING WARM-UP.** What are some things people can do to improve their appearance?

B 🎧 **READING.** Read the magazine article about cosmetic surgery. Do you think people should consider these solutions to their problems?

Cosmetic surgery— for everyone?

Cosmetic surgeons have made great progress in restoring normal appearance by repairing injuries and removing scars from burns and other injuries. More and more, however, many people with the necessary financial resources have chosen cosmetic surgery—an expensive option—to improve their appearance. Gail Weiss, *Fitness and Health Magazine*'s medical editor, answers readers' questions about cosmetic surgery.

BEFORE cosmetic surgery **AFTER** cosmetic surgery

Dear Dr. Weiss:
When I was young, I was a chocoholic. I ate a lot of chocolate, but I never gained any weight. Now that I'm older, I can't eat anything without gaining weight! I've heard that liposuction is the answer to an overweight person's dreams. What's up with that?
Dawson

Dear Dawson:
It's true that liposuction can remove fat deposits that don't respond to dieting and exercise, but it's expensive and can be dangerous. It would be a good idea to ask your doctor for some help in dieting first. Then, if you are unsuccessful, be sure to find a surgeon with a lot of experience before deciding on liposuction.
Gail Weiss, M.D.

Dear Dr. Weiss:
I'm a 24-year-old man who is already losing his hair! Dr. Weiss, I'm looking for a wife and I'm afraid no woman will want to marry a 25-year-old baldie! I need some advice.
Calvin

Dear Calvin:
There are several surgical procedures which a cosmetic surgeon can perform to help treat hair loss and restore hair for both men and women. But if that's not practical, remember that some of the world's most attractive men are bald!
Gail Weiss, M.D.

Dear Dr. Weiss:
Can anyone help me with my problem? I have too much hair on my body and I'm sick and tired of shaving. It's so embarrassing.
Cassandra

Dear Cassandra:
Before you call a cosmetic surgeon for hair removal, try a depilatory cream. Depilatories are available in any drugstore and they remove hair easily and safely in your own home. Why don't you give that a try first?
Gail Weiss, M.D.

Dear Dr. Weiss:
I'm at my wits' end with my face. I have wrinkles and sun damage. I'm only 30, but I look 50. Do you think a face-lift is an option for me?
Josephine

Dear Josephine:
Both men and women of all ages request this popular and effective surgery. It lifts the face and the neck in one operation and has excellent results. But this is surgery, and afterwards you will have to stay at home for a number of days. It takes time to recover. And you may have to do it again after a number of years. Before you decide to have a face-lift, ask your dermatologist or a cosmetic surgeon about a chemical peel. A chemical peel removes the top layer of skin and can improve the appearance of the skin without surgery. Good luck!
Gail Weiss, M.D.

INFORMATION SOURCE:
American Academy of Cosmetic Surgery
http://www.cosmeticsurgery.org

C PAIR WORK. Complete the chart with information from the article. Explain your answers.

	Problem	Dr. Weiss's advice
Dawson	*overweight*	*diet first*
Calvin		
Cassandra		
Josephine		

INTERACTION • *Would you ever get a face-lift?*

STEP 1. Take the personal opinion survey about ways to improve appearance.

Would you try...?

	definitely	maybe	probably not	absolutely not!
diet	○	○	○	○
exercise	○	○	○	○
massage	○	○	○	○
creams and lotions	○	○	○	○
hair removal	○	○	○	○
hair restoration	○	○	○	○
makeup	○	○	○	○
facials	○	○	○	○
face-lifts	○	○	○	○
liposuction	○	○	○	○
chemical peels	○	○	○	○

STEP 2. PAIR WORK. Choose one method you would try and one method you would not try. On the notepad, write advantages and disadvantages. Compare your notepad with a partner's.

method	advantage(s)	disadvantage(s)
I would try diet.	free, safe	hard to do!

STEP 3. DISCUSSION. What's the best way to improve appearance?

STEP 4. WRITING. Write a letter to Dr. Weiss. Then exchange letters with your partner and write a response.

FREE PRACTICE

UNIT 5
CHECKPOINT

A 🎧 **LISTENING COMPREHENSION.** **Listen carefully to the conversations.**
Complete the statements.

1. Hawaii Bronzer is a brand of _____.
2. Swan is a brand of _____.
3. Truly You is a brand of _____.
4. Mountain Fresh is a brand of _____.
5. Silk 'n' Satin is a brand of _____.

B **Give advice to each person.**

1. "My nails are a mess!"

   YOU *You should get a manicure* _____.

2. "Just look at my hair! What should I do?"

   YOU _____.

3. "Oh, my aching back! I played tennis and then I cleaned the house."

   YOU _____.

C **Complete each statement or question.**

1. There aren't _____ customers in the store right now.

many / much

2. Do they have _____ good shampoo at the spa?

any / many

3. Your sister doesn't want _____ conditioner.

some / any

4. You don't have _____ makeup in the bathroom.

much / some

5. My son uses _____ razor blades.

any / a lot of

6. It's not good to give children _____ cough medicine.

some / a lot of

D **Choose a response to each question.**

1. "Facials are two for the price of one. Feel like getting a facial with me?"
   a. It's not customary to tip.   b. I think I'll pass.

2. "Can I get a manicure in the meantime?"
   a. Actually, we don't have many.   b. Certainly. Right over there.

3. "How much do you charge for a shave and a haircut?"
   a. You can charge it to your room.   b. I'm not sure. Let me check.

E **WRITING.** **On a separate sheet of paper, write about a personal care product you like. What does it do for you? Why do you buy it?**

> I've used Scrubbie Toothpaste since I was a child. First of
> all, it tastes great. It's also a very popular...

TOP NOTCH PROJECT
Bring in ads for cosmetics and makeup. What do the ads say they can do to improve appearance? Make a bulletin board of products.

TOP NOTCH WEBSITE
For Unit 5 online activites, visit the *Top Notch* Companion Website at www.longman.com/topnotch.

Medicine	1	Hair Care	3
Makeup	2	Shaving	3
Nail Care	2	Skin Care	4
Tooth Care	2		

UNIT WRAP-UP

- **Vocabulary.** Name the personal care products you see. Make a list of other products you think you can find in the store.

- **Grammar.** Make statements with <u>some</u>, <u>any</u>, <u>many</u>, <u>much</u>, and <u>a lot of</u>.

  There's a lot of makeup in the store.

- **Social language.** Go shopping. Ask the clerk for products.

Aisle 2

Aisle 3

✓ Now I can ...

- ☐ ask for something I can't find.
- ☐ request salon services.
- ☐ schedule and pay for personal care.
- ☐ discuss ways to improve appearance.

61

Eating Well

UNIT GOALS
1 Make an excuse to decline food
2 Talk about food passions
3 Discuss lifestyle changes
4 Describe unique foods

A TOPIC PREVIEW. Look at the Healthy-Eating Pyramid that suggests daily eating habits to avoid heart disease. Is there anything in the pyramid that you <u>never</u> eat?

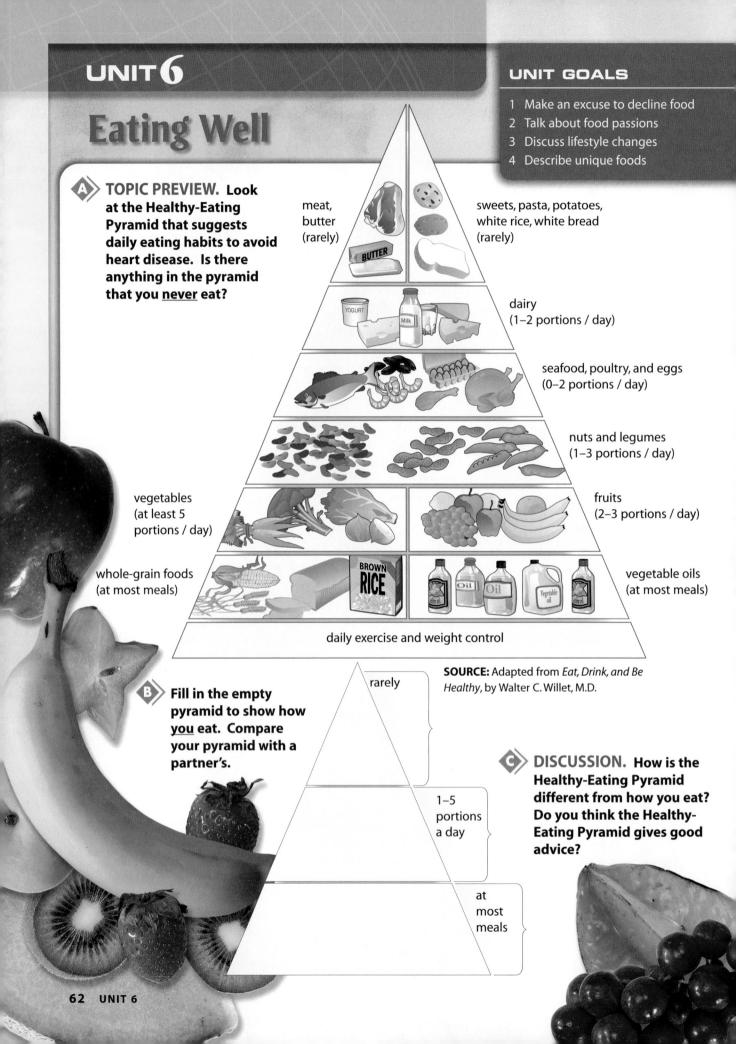

meat, butter (rarely)

BUTTER

sweets, pasta, potatoes, white rice, white bread (rarely)

dairy (1–2 portions / day)

seafood, poultry, and eggs (0–2 portions / day)

nuts and legumes (1–3 portions / day)

vegetables (at least 5 portions / day)

fruits (2–3 portions / day)

whole-grain foods (at most meals)

BROWN RICE

Oil Oil Vegetable oil

vegetable oils (at most meals)

daily exercise and weight control

SOURCE: Adapted from *Eat, Drink, and Be Healthy*, by Walter C. Willet, M.D.

B Fill in the empty pyramid to show how <u>you</u> eat. Compare your pyramid with a partner's.

rarely

1–5 portions a day

at most meals

C DISCUSSION. How is the Healthy-Eating Pyramid different from how you eat? Do you think the Healthy-Eating Pyramid gives good advice?

D 🎧 **SOUND BITES.** Read along silently as you listen to a natural conversation.

IRIS: What in the world are you eating?
TERRI: Chocolate cake. But don't tell anyone, OK?
IRIS: But aren't you on a diet?
TERRI: I used to be. Not anymore.
IRIS: What happened?
TERRI: To tell you the truth, it was just too much trouble.

TERRI: Want to try some?
IRIS: Well, I would. But I'm on a diet.
TERRI: You? I don't believe it! Don't you always have dessert?
IRIS: I used to. Not anymore.
TERRI: Are you sure? You only live once!

E Check the statements that are true, according to the conversation.
Explain your answers.

☐ **1.** Iris doesn't eat sweets now.
☐ **2.** Terri doesn't eat sweets now.
☐ **3.** Iris doesn't want any cake.

☐ **4.** Terri doesn't want any cake.
☐ **5.** Iris changed her eating habits.
☐ **6.** Terri changed her eating habits.

WHAT ABOUT **YOU?**

Make a list of foods you can eat if …

| **you're trying to lose weight.** |
| |
| |
| |
| **you're trying to gain weight.** |
| |
| |
| |

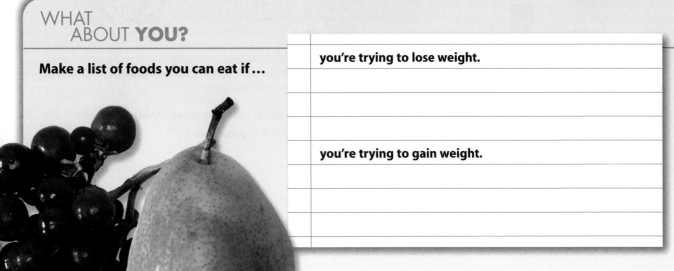

Make an Excuse to Decline Food

CONVERSATION MODEL Read and listen.

A: Everything's ready. Why don't we sit down?
B: This food looks great!
C: It really smells delicious.

• • •

A: Please help yourself.
C: Thanks. But I'll pass on the chicken.
A: Don't you eat chicken?
C: Actually, no. I'm a vegetarian.
A: I'm sorry. I didn't know that.
C: Don't worry about it. It's not a problem.

Rhythm and intonation practice

A **VOCABULARY.** Excuses for not eating something. Listen and practice.

I **don't care for** broccoli.

Coffee **doesn't agree with me**.

I'm **a vegetarian**.

I'm **on a diet**. / I'm **trying to lose weight**.

I'm **avoiding** sugar.

I'm **allergic to** chocolate.

B **LISTENING COMPREHENSION.** Listen carefully to each conversation. Write the letter to complete each statement. Then listen again to check your work.

_____ **1.** Cindy   **a.** is a vegetarian.

_____ **2.** Frankie   **b.** is avoiding salt and oil.

_____ **3.** Marie   **c.** is trying to lose weight.

_____ **4.** Susan   **d.** is allergic to strawberries.

_____ **5.** George   **e.** doesn't care for fish.

GRAMMAR. Negative <u>yes</u> / <u>no</u> questions and <u>Why don't</u>...?

Use negative <u>yes</u> / <u>no</u> questions...

• **to check information you think is true.**

Isn't Jane a vegetarian?	Yes, she is.
Don't they have two sons?	No, they don't. They have three.

• **when you want someone to agree with you.**

Don't you love Italian food?	Yes. It's delicious.
Wasn't that a terrible dinner?	Actually, I disagree. I liked it.

• **to express surprise.**

Aren't you going to have cake?	I'm sorry. I'm on a diet.
Hasn't he finished eating yet?	I know. Kevin's a very slow eater.

Use statements with <u>Why don't</u> ...? to make an offer or a suggestion.

Why don't you have some more cake?	Thanks.
Why don't we go out to eat?	Good idea.

GRAMMAR BOOSTER

PAGES G10–G11
For more ...

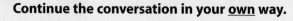 **Complete each negative <u>yes</u> / <u>no</u> question.**

1. **A:** _____ you allergic to seafood?

   B: Me? No. You're thinking of my brother.

2. **A:** _____ you like your salad?

   B: Not really. It was too spicy for me.

3. **A:** _____ that dinner last night delicious?

   B: It was fantastic!

4. **A:** _____ you already made roast chicken this week?

   B: Yes. Don't you like it?

CONVERSATION
PAIR WORK

Role-play a dinner with friends. Use the pictures and make excuses to decline food.

A: Why don't you help yourself?
B: Thanks. But I'll pass on _____.
A: Don't you _____?
B: _____ ...

Continue the conversation in your <u>own</u> way.

DISCUSSION. Are there any foods you won't eat? Why not?

sardines

chocolates

shellfish

tofu

steak

noodles

fries

CONTROLLED PRACTICE

2 *Talk about Food Passions*

🎧 CONVERSATION **MODEL** **Read and listen.**

A: Have you tried the coffee? It's terrific!

B: No, thanks. Are you a big coffee drinker?

A: Definitely. I'm crazy about coffee. What about you?

B: I used to have it a lot. But I've been cutting back.

A: Well, I couldn't live without it.

🎧 **Rhythm and intonation practice**

A 🎧 **VOCABULARY.** Food passions. **Listen and practice.**

I'm **crazy about** seafood!
I'm **a big** meat **eater**.
I'm **a big** coffee **drinker**.
I'm **a chocolate addict**.
I'm **a pizza lover**.

I **can't stand** fish!
I'm **not crazy about** chocolate.
I **don't care for** steak.
I'm **not much of a** pizza **eater**.
I'm **not much of a** coffee **drinker**.

B 🎧 **LISTENING COMPREHENSION.** **Listen carefully to each speaker and check the statements that are true. Then listen again to check your work.**

1. **a.** ☐ She's crazy about sushi.   **b.** ☐ She can't stand sushi.
2. **a.** ☐ He's not crazy about asparagus.   **b.** ☐ He loves asparagus.
3. **a.** ☐ She's a mango lover.   **b.** ☐ She doesn't care for mangoes.
4. **a.** ☐ He's a big pasta eater.   **b.** ☐ He isn't crazy about pasta.
5. **a.** ☐ She can't stand ice cream.   **b.** ☐ She's an ice cream addict.

sushi

asparagus

mangoes

pasta

ice cream

C **PAIR WORK.** **Use the vocabulary to tell your partner about <u>your</u> food passions.**

D GRAMMAR. Used to

Use <u>used to</u> and the base form of a verb for habitual actions in the past that are not true now.

My daughter **used to love** candy. But now she doesn't care for it.

I **didn't use to eat** vegetables. But now I'm crazy about them.

Questions and answers

Didn't Mary **use to avoid** sweets?   Yes, she did. / No, she didn't.

What did you **use to eat** for breakfast?   Eggs and sausage. But not anymore.

| I you he / she they we | **used** to didn't **use** to |

GRAMMAR BOOSTER

PAGE G12
For more ...

E 🎧 PRONUNCIATION. <u>Used to</u>. Notice how /tu/ often reduces to /tə/ in <u>used to</u>. Listen and repeat.

1. I used to eat fatty foods.

2. Jack used to like sweets.

3. Sally used to be a vegetarian.

4. I used to like seafood.

F Complete each sentence logically with <u>used to</u> or <u>didn't use to</u>.

1. Tom _____ eat a lot of fatty foods. But now he avoids them.

2. Carol _____ hate fish. But now she's crazy about it.

3. Arthur _____ have vegetables. But now he has them all the time.

4. Victor _____ drink a lot of coffee. But now he doesn't care for it very much.

5. Nancy _____ eat many sweets. But now she does.

6. Fran _____ go out to restaurants a lot. But now she eats at home more often.

G PAIR WORK. Ask your partner questions about things he or she used to do but doesn't do now.

CONVERSATION
PAIR WORK

Complete the chart with foods you like and dislike. Then role-play a dinner party conversation about food passions with a partner. Use the guide, or create a new conversation.

A: Have you tried the _____? _____ terrific!

B: No, thanks. Are you _____?

A: _____. What about you?

B: _____ ...

Continue the conversation in your <u>own</u> way.

Foods I'm crazy about	Foods I can't stand

CONTROLLED PRACTICE

Discuss Lifestyle Changes

A **READING WARM-UP.** Do you think people's eating habits are better or worse than they used to be?

B 🎧 **READING.** Read the article. Use the glossary for new words.

Changing Lifestyles Contribute to Obesity

Seth Mydans, *The New York Times*

Around the world, more than one billion adults are overweight, and at least 300 million of these are classified as obese. While this used to be a problem primarily in the West, the number of obese Asians has been increasing dramatically. Obesity is spreading throughout Asia, especially among children, as people move to big cities, where they eat fattier fast foods and live a more sedentary lifestyle.

"We spoil him," says Warisa Waid, a teacher in Bangkok, Thailand, of her 11-year-old son, Saharat. "We don't care if it is good or bad; we just feed him whatever he wants." She adds, "He spends most of his time in front of the TV, playing video games and watching cartoons."

When Saharat was younger, he was small for his age. "His father's family believes that being skinny is bad, so they kept telling me, 'Why don't you feed your kid more?' and, 'What's wrong with him?' His grandparents give him fast food, pizza, and all that." She adds, "He loves deep-fried stuff, and he doesn't eat vegetables at all."

In Asian cities, processed foods and fast foods rich with sugar and saturated fats are often the most available and the cheapest. At the same time, people are getting less physical exercise. Dr. Augusto D. Litonjua of the Philippines blames what he calls "malling," which he defines as spending the day in shopping malls and eating at fast-food restaurants.

Milk, ice cream, cookies, soft drinks, and potato chips—once all foreign foods—are as common in many parts of Asia now as in the West. People are eating more meat and eggs and less rice and vegetables. In the last two decades, Thais have doubled their annual intake of sugar.

The World Health Organization (WHO) reports that 6 out of 10 deaths in the region are due to diseases that may be linked to obesity—heart attacks, stroke, diabetes, hypertension, and some forms of cancer.

SOURCE: Adapted by permission from *The New York Times*

GLOSSARY

sedentary not active

processed foods foods that are not fresh; e.g., frozen or canned

heart attack sudden damage to the heart because the blood flow is blocked

stroke damage caused when an artery in the brain stops working

diabetes a disease in which there is too much sugar in the blood

hypertension high blood pressure

cancer a disease which produces a growth that can cause death

C Check the statements that are true, according to the article. Explain your answers.

☐ **1.** Obesity is a new health problem in Asia.

☐ **2.** Saharat Waid is on a diet now.

☐ **3.** Many Asians are going to exercise classes in malls.

☐ **4.** Asians are eating foods today that they didn't use to eat.

☐ **5.** Obesity is not a serious problem.

D **DISCUSSION.**

1. How are people's lifestyles in your city similar to those described in the article? How are they different?

2. What advice would you give Warisa Waid?

STEP 1. GROUP WORK. Complete the class
survey and discuss the results.

Lifestyle Survey

1. How many students have ever tried some kind of a diet to lose weight? What diets have they tried?	2. How many students have changed the way they eat to avoid illness? How?	3. How many students lead an active, non-sedentary lifestyle? What do they do?
No. of students _____	No. of students _____	No. of students _____
Examples	Examples	Examples
☐ ate less food	☐ don't eat sugar	☐ work out in a gym
☐ avoided desserts	☐ don't eat fast foods	☐ play sports
☐ avoided fatty foods	☐ eat whole grains	☐ walk or run
☐ other _____	☐ other _____	☐ other _____

Total number of students in the class [ ]

STEP 2. PAIR WORK. On your notepad, write some positive and negative
lifestyle changes you have made in your life. Then compare your
notes with a partner's. Talk about how your eating and exercise
habits have changed in your life.

> ❝I didn't use to go to a gym, but now I do. That was a positive change.❞

Some positive changes	Some negative changes

STEP 3. DISCUSSION. How have most people's eating
and exercise habits changed over the last 20 years?

> ❝People are eating a lot more fast foods. I don't think that's a good thing.❞

STEP 4. WRITING. Write about how people's lifestyles
have changed for the better or worse.

Describe Unique Foods

A ○ VOCABULARY. Food descriptions. Listen and practice.

It looks terrific.

It smells terrible.

It tastes { sweet. spicy. salty. sour.

**It smells like
It tastes like** } chicken.
It looks like

It's { **soft. hard.**

It's { **chewy. crunchy.**

B ○ LISTENING COMPREHENSION. First, listen to descriptions of foods from around the world and write the letter of each food. Then listen again and use the vocabulary to complete each description.

☑ 1. It's _chewy_, and it tastes _sweet_.

☐ 2. It tastes _____, and it's _____.

☐ 3. It's _____, and it tastes _____.

☐ 4. It tastes _____. Some think it looks _____.

☐ 5. It tastes _____, and it smells _____.

☐ 6. They're _____, and they're _____.

a kim chee / Korea cabbage

b chapulines / Mexico grasshopper

c mochi / Japan

d Vegemite® / Australia

e Jell-O® / United States

f cho dofu / China

TOP NOTCH
INTERACTION • *Does it taste good?*

STEP 1. Choose three foods that you would like to serve a visitor to your country. Write notes about each food.

Name of food:
fried cheese balls

Description:
salty, chewy

What's in it?
cheese, flour, oil

Name of food:
_____

Description:
_____

What's in it?
_____

Name of food:
_____

Description:
_____

What's in it?
_____

Name of food:
_____

Description:
_____

What's in it?
_____

STEP 2. GROUP WORK. In small groups, role-play a dinner party. One student plays the role of the host. The others are the guests.

NEED HELP? **Here's language you already know:**

Host
Everything's ready.
Why don't we sit down?
Please help yourself.
Would you like some _____?
Why don't you have some more _____?
Don't you eat / drink _____?

Guest
What's in it? Is it [spicy]?
I'm a _____ addict / lover.
I'm a big _____ eater / drinker.
I'm crazy about _____.
I don't care for _____.
I'm a vegetarian.
I'm allergic to _____.
_____ doesn't agree with me.
I'm avoiding _____.

Guest
The _____ is / are terrific.
I'm trying to lose weight. / I'm on a diet.
I'll pass on the _____.
I used to eat _____, but not anymore.

STEP 3. WRITING. Write a description of one of the dishes at your dinner party. Use the questions as a guide.

Is it an appetizer? An entrée? A dessert?
When do people eat it? Every day? On holidays?
When was the first time you tried it?

FREE PRACTICE

71

UNIT 6
CHECKPOINT

A 🎧 **LISTENING COMPREHENSION.** **Listen and check the foods that each person likes and dislikes.**

	shrimp	clams	fish	steak	pasta	chicken	carrots
1. He's crazy about …	☐	☐	☐	☐	☐	☐	☐
He doesn't care for …	☐	☐	☐	☐	☐	☐	☐
2. She's crazy about …	☐	☐	☐	☐	☐	☐	☐
She doesn't care for …	☐	☐	☐	☐	☐	☐	☐

B **Complete a negative yes / no question for each situation.**

1. You see a woman on the street. You're pretty sure she's Joan Chen, the famous Chinese actress. You go up to her and ask her: "_Aren't you_ Joan Chen?"

2. You are walking with a friend. You're pretty sure you see Michael Jordan, the famous basketball player, walking across the street. You ask your friend: "_____ Michael Jordan?"

3. You and your friend went out for dinner. Unfortunately, the meal was very bad. After you leave, you say to your friend: "_____ the food awful?"

4. You and your friend enjoyed a day at the park yesterday. You thought the weather was really beautiful. You say to your friend: "_____ the weather beautiful?"

5. Your new classmate is eating lunch at 3:00 p.m. You are surprised because it's so late. You say to your classmate: "_____ lunch yet?"

C **Write five sentences about things you did or didn't do when you were younger. Use used to or didn't use to.**

1. _____ .
2. _____ .
3. _____ .
4. _____ .
5. _____ .

D **Describe the following foods in your own way.**

Example: carrots _They're orange and they're sweet and crunchy_ .

1. squid (or octopus) _____ .
2. ice cream _____ .
3. bananas _____ .
4. cabbage _____ .
5. steak _____ .

> **TOP NOTCH PROJECT**
> Find articles about food and health in your local newspapers or magazines. Discuss them with your class.

> **TOP NOTCH WEBSITE**
> For Unit 6 online activities, visit the *Top Notch* Companion Website at www.longman.com/topnotch.

UNIT WRAP-UP

- **Grammar.** Write five negative <u>yes</u> / <u>no</u> questions.
  Doesn't the chicken look delicious?

- **Social language.** Look at the dishes and the ingredients. Then role-play conversations with a partner about the food.

International Buffet
TODAY'S SELECTIONS

"Caramel Apple" / United States

Ingredients:
apples, butter, brown sugar, nuts

"Beef and Broccoli" / China

Ingredients:
beef, red peppers, peanut oil, garlic, broccoli, onions, mushrooms

"Rain Doughnuts" / Brazil

Ingredients:
flour, milk, eggs, sugar, oil

"Bi Bim Bop" / Korea

Ingredients:
rice, beef, soy sauce, sesame oil, garlic, black pepper, salt, eggs, lettuce, rice wine, hot pepper sauce

"Pad Thai" / Thailand

Ingredients:
rice noodles, chicken, tofu, peanuts, fish sauce, sugar, lime juice, vegetable oil, garlic, shrimp, eggs, hot peppers

"Arepas" / Venezuela

Ingredients:
corn flour, salt, white cheese, oil

"Chicken Mole" / Mexico

Ingredients:
chicken, salt, vegetable oil, onions, garlic, tomatoes, chocolate

✔ *Now I can ...*

- ☐ make an excuse to decline food.
- ☐ talk about food passions.
- ☐ discuss lifestyle changes.
- ☐ describe unique foods.

Psychology and Personality

UNIT GOALS

1 Discuss color preferences
2 Cheer someone up
3 Determine your personality type
4 Discuss the impact of birth order
  on personality

A **TOPIC PREVIEW.** Is color important to you? Do colors have meanings? Take the color survey.

1. tomato red	2. berry red	3. deep red	4. red-purple	5. mauve	6. pink	7. fuchsia
8. purple	9. light purple	10. blue-purple	11. blue	12. medium light blue	13. light blue	14. dark blue
15. blue-green	16. deep blue-green	17. green	18. emerald green	19. lime green	20. light green	21. dark green
22. dark yellow-green	23. muted yellow-green	24. yellow-green	25. yellow	26. dark yellow	27. yellow-orange	28. light yellow
29. orange	30. pink-orange	31. light orange	32. brown	33. orange-brown	34. golden brown	35. light brown
36. white	37. cream	38. black	39. dark gray	40. gray	41. blue-gray	
42. silver	43. platinum	44. gold				

Please let us know what you think about color! Eight easy questions! There are no wrong answers. Use the color chart. You can use the same color more than once!

1 Which is your **favorite** color? _____

2 Which is your **least favorite** color? _____

3 Which color do you associate with **happiness**? _____

4 Which color do you associate with **purity**? _____

5 Which color do you associate with **good luck**? _____

6 Which color do you associate with **death**? _____

7 Which color do you associate with **power**? _____

8 Which color or color combinations are **bad luck**? _____

SOURCE: Adapted from the Color Matters® Global Color Survey http://express.colorcom.com

B **DISCUSSION.** Where do you think color preferences come from: our culture or our own individual tastes?

C 🎧 **SOUND BITES.** **Read along silently as you listen to a natural conversation.**

TRACY: So what do you feel like doing after dinner?
SARAH: I don't know. You decide. I'm kind of down in the dumps.

TRACY: You do look a little blue. Something wrong?
SARAH: Nothing I can put my finger on. I guess I'm just feeling a little out of sorts since I got back from vacation.
TRACY: Maybe a nice dinner will cheer you up.

D **UNDERSTAND MEANING FROM CONTEXT.** **Complete each statement, according to the conversation.**

1. When Sarah says she's "kind of down in the dumps," she means _____.
   a. She's feeling sad.   **b.** She's feeling happy.

2. When Tracy tells Sarah she looks "a little blue," she means _____.
   a. Sarah looks sad.   **b.** Sarah looks happy.

3. When Sarah says she's feeling "a little out of sorts," she means _____.
   a. She's feeling sad.   **b.** She's feeling happy.

E **PAIR WORK.** **Answer the questions together.**

1. What's Sarah's problem?

2. What does Tracy suggest?

WHAT
ABOUT **YOU?**

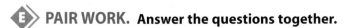

Answer each question. Then compare your answers with a partner's.

1. What makes you feel blue? _____

2. What cheers you up when you're down in the dumps? _____

3. What do you do to help a friend who's feeling down? _____

Discuss Color Preferences

🎧 CONVERSATION
MODEL **Read and listen.**

A: You know, I'd like to repaint the kitchen.

B: OK. What color?

A: How about gray?

B: Well, I don't mind repainting it, but gray's out of the question.

A: Why? What's wrong with gray?

B: It's boring.

A: Really? To me, gray's calm, not boring.

🎧 **Rhythm and intonation practice**

> **Gerund:** an -ing form of a verb (painting)
>
> **Infinitive:** to + a base form (to paint)

A **GRAMMAR.** **Gerunds and infinitives after certain verbs**

Gerunds

She enjoys **painting**.

They discussed **going** on vacation.

Infinitives

He wants **to paint** the bedroom red.

I decided **to exercise** more often.

Use a gerund after the following verbs: avoid, can't stand, discuss, dislike, enjoy, feel like, (don't) mind, practice, quit, suggest.

Use an infinitive after the following verbs: agree, be sure, choose, decide, expect, hope, learn, need, plan, seem, want, wish, would like.

GRAMMAR BOOSTER

PAGES G13–G14
For more …

B **Complete the advice for the "blues." Use gerunds and infinitives.**

Learn to be your own best friend!

Everybody feels a little blue from time to time. If you _____

1. not feel like / talk
about it and you _____ advice books, here are some helpful

2. dislike / read
hints. First of all, _____ your health. _____ coffee

3. decide / take care of 4. Avoid / drink
and alcohol. Exercise can be very helpful. If you _____, I

5. choose / exercise
_____ with a friend you _____ with. _____

6. suggest / go 7. enjoy / laugh 8. Be sure / eat
right and, importantly, _____ lots of sleep. If you _____

9. be sure / get 10. would like / take
a day off from work and you _____ to the movies or

11. want / go
_____ a walk in the park, just do it. _____ yourself

12. plan / take 13. Learn / cheer
up. You can be your own best friend! Oh, and a final note: Everybody finds

certain colors "happy." Try to wear the colors <u>you</u> find most cheerful.

◯ **PRONUNCIATION.** Reduction of <u>to</u> in infinitive phrases. **Notice how unstressed <u>to</u> reduces to /tə/. Listen and repeat.**

1. I decided to repaint the bedroom.
2. She needs to get lots of sleep.
3. We plan to drive downtown tomorrow.
4. I know you'd like to travel more.

◆ ◯ **VOCABULARY.** Adjectives of emotion. **Listen and practice.**

positive emotions

a **happy** event   an **exciting** game   a **cheerful** scene   a **calm** child

negative emotions

a **sad** occasion   a **depressing** day   a **disgusting** scene   a **nervous** person

◆ ◯ **LISTENING COMPREHENSION.** **Listen to the conversations. Then complete each statement with the color and the adjective of emotion.**

1. He thinks _____ is a _____ color.
2. She thinks the _____ suit will be _____.
3. He thinks the _____ chair will make him _____.
4. She doesn't like _____ shoes. She thinks they're _____.

CONVERSATION
PAIR WORK

Discuss repainting a room or buying a new car, new clothes, shoes, or something else. Compare tastes in color. Use the guide, or create a new conversation.

A: You know, I'd like to _____.

B: _____. What color?

A: How about _____?

B: _____ …

Continue the conversation in your <u>own</u> way.

CONTROLLED PRACTICE

Cheer Someone Up

∩ CONVERSATION MODEL Read and listen.

A: You look down. What's up?

B: Oh, nothing serious. I'm just tired of the same old grind. But thanks for asking.

A: I know what you mean. I'm tired of working, too. How about going to a movie?

B: Great idea. Let's go!

∩ Rhythm and intonation practice

 GRAMMAR. Gerunds after prepositions

You can use a gerund as the object of a preposition.

	preposition	object
We can go to a movie instead	of	watching TV.
Thanks	for	asking.
They believe	in	being honest.

Don't use an infinitive as the object of a preposition.

(NOT We can go to a movie instead of ~~to watch TV.~~)

adjective + preposition

angry about	afraid of
excited about	sick / tired of
happy / sad about	bored with

verb + preposition

complain about	apologize for
talk about	believe in
worry about	object to

GRAMMAR BOOSTER

PAGE G14
For more ...

 B Complete the descriptions of Ted and Nicole with prepositions and gerunds.

Ted is an extrovert. Like most extroverts, he's direct. And he's honest; he believes _____ the truth.
1. tell

At his job, he works with other people and he never complains _____ long
2. work
hours. He doesn't worry _____ work on weekends
3. have to
or holidays.

He has a few fears, though. Most of all, he's afraid _____.
4. fly

Ted's wife, Nicole, on the other hand, is an introvert. But she doesn't object _____ about herself from time to time.
5. talk

Right now, she's bored _____ a student, and she's sick and tired _____ so many long reports and _____ exams every few weeks! She's angry _____ spend so much time in front of a computer.
6. be
7. write
8. take
9. have to

But she's excited _____ on vacation. Unlike Ted, she's not at all afraid _____!
10. go
11. fly

C ▷ **PAIR WORK. Fill out the form for yourself, using gerunds. Then share information with a partner.**

> " Right now, I'm happy about getting engaged! "

Right now, what are you . . .
happy about? _____
excited about? _____
bored with? _____
sick and tired of? _____

CONVERSATION
PAIR WORK

Role-play cheering someone up. Use the guide and suggestions, or create a new conversation.

A: You look _____. What's up?

B: Oh, nothing serious. I'm just tired of _____. But thanks for asking.

A: I know what you mean. _____.

B: _____.

💡 **Suggestions ...**

- Why don't we [go for a walk]?
- Maybe a [vacation] would cheer you up.
- Would you like me to [make you some soup]?
- How about some [ice cream]? That always makes me feel better!
- Your own suggestion

3 Determine Your Personality Type

A 🎧 **LISTENING COMPREHENSION. Listen to the discussion between a professor and his students. What's the subject of the conversation?**

B 🎧 **Listen again and check the statements that are true, according to the professor.**

☐ **1.** Not everyone has a personality.

☐ **2.** A person's personality includes the usual behavior, thoughts, and emotions of that person.

☐ **3.** Emotions and thoughts are the same thing.

☐ **4.** The word "emotion" is similar in meaning to the word "feeling."

☐ **5.** The people in a family almost always have similar personalities.

☐ **6.** Personality comes only from the environment.

C **Match each word with an explanation from the discussion. Listen again, if necessary, to check your answers.**

_____ **1.** personality   **a.** everything you learn from: family, culture, and life experiences

_____ **2.** thoughts   **b.** another word for genetics in discussing personality

_____ **3.** emotions   **c.** traits that come from the parents

_____ **4.** genetics   **d.** feelings, such as love, anger, fear, and hate

_____ **5.** the environment   **e.** a person's pattern or style of behavior

_____ **6.** nature   **f.** memories, wishes, and plans

_____ **7.** nurture   **g.** another word for environment in discussing personality

D **DISCUSSION. Where do you think you got your personality—more from "nature" or more from "nurture"?**

STEP 1. **Determine your personality type.** **Find out if you are an introvert or an extrovert by completing the following survey.**

ARE YOU AN INTROVERT OR AN EXTROVERT?

Instructions: From each pair of personality traits, check one that sounds like <u>your</u> personality. At the end, add up your selections for each column. Then decide for yourself: Are you an introvert or an extrovert?

	Extroverts tend to:	Introverts tend to:
1.	○ enjoy being in a group.	○ enjoy being alone.
2.	○ need to interact with others.	○ avoid interacting unnecessarily.
3.	○ be active.	○ be quiet.
4.	○ be interested in events.	○ be interested in feelings.
5.	○ sometimes talk without thinking.	○ usually think without talking.
6.	○ be easy to "understand."	○ be hard to know.
7.	○ know many people a little.	○ know few people, but well.
8.	○ talk.	○ listen.
9.	○ seek excitement.	○ seek peace.
10.	○ say what they mean.	○ keep their ideas to themselves.

Total extrovert selections ○   Total introvert selections ○

○ **I'm an extrovert.**   ○ **I'm an introvert.**   ○ **I'm a mixture of both!**

SOURCE: Excerpted and adapted from "Discover your personality type" <u>www.win.net</u>

STEP 2. **GROUP WORK.** **Talk about the personality traits you checked.**
Find a real example from your life to explain.

> " I'm an extrovert. I like to sing for people and act in plays. "

STEP 3. **WRITING.** **Write about your own personality. Talk about your personality traits. Explain whether you are an introvert or an extrovert. Give examples and reasons.**

> I'm an extrovert, just like my father. I am talkative, open and honest, and I dislike
> being alone. I have a lot of friends, and I love going out with them in a large group . . .

4 Discuss the Impact of Birth Order on Personality

A ▸ READING WARM-UP. Do you think the first child in a family has different personality traits from children who are born later?

B ▸ 🎧 READING. Read the article. Which description sounds like **your** personality?

BirthOrder
RELATIONSHIPS

When did you arrive in your family? Are you the oldest child, a middle child, or the "baby"? Birth order may not be the <u>most</u> important factor in personality development, but we can make some generalizations.

If you're the OLDEST, you're probably:

- successful.
- conservative.
- self-critical—always feeling you could do better.
- able to enjoy the company of older people.

Parents often expect a lot from the first child. They often push them to succeed. The first child often has to grow up very fast.

If you're a MIDDLE child, you're probably:

- the one with the most friends.
- the silent rebel against the family's values.

Middle children often feel less important than their older or younger siblings.

If you're the YOUNGEST child, you're probably:

- a show-off who enjoys the limelight.
- often the family clown, making everyone laugh.
- both charming and a rebel—lovable one minute and breaking rules the next.
- creative in art, music, and other ways.

The youngest child often has the longest childhood.

SOURCE: Theresa M. Campbell www.suite101.com

C ▸ Find these words in the article. Then complete each statement with one of the words.

clown
values
self-critical
creative
charming
rebel
sibling

1. Another word for a brother or a sister is a _____.
2. The cultural rules within each family are its _____.
3. Another word for lovable is _____.
4. People who feel they should "do better" are _____.
5. A person who doesn't follow the rules is a _____.
6. Artists, musical composers, and writers are _____.
7. A person who enjoys making other people laugh is a _____.

D ▸ DISCUSSION. In families you know, are the descriptions in the article generally true? Give examples to support your opinion.

STEP 1. Fill out the checklist for yourself.

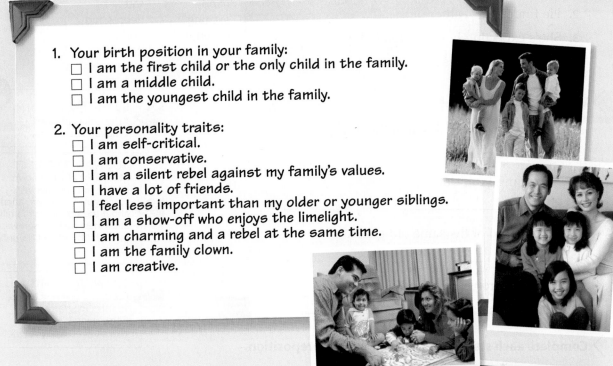

1. Your birth position in your family:
   ☐ I am the first child or the only child in the family.
   ☐ I am a middle child.
   ☐ I am the youngest child in the family.

2. Your personality traits:
   ☐ I am self-critical.
   ☐ I am conservative.
   ☐ I am a silent rebel against my family's values.
   ☐ I have a lot of friends.
   ☐ I feel less important than my older or younger siblings.
   ☐ I am a show-off who enjoys the limelight.
   ☐ I am charming and a rebel at the same time.
   ☐ I am the family clown.
   ☐ I am creative.

STEP 2. GROUP WORK. Form three groups of students, according to your birth positions:

- group 1: first or only children
- group 2: middle children
- group 3: youngest children ["the babies"]

Compare your checklists with other members of your group. Do you share the same personality traits?

STEP 3. First children are often the most successful in life. On your notepad, write one or more reasons why you think this happens. Some possibilities: nature, nurture, parents.

STEP 4. DISCUSSION. How does birth order affect a person's chances for success in life? Can someone's personality change?

A 🎧 **LISTENING COMPREHENSION. Listen to the conversations. Then complete each statement with one or more of the adjectives.**

1. She prefers _____ music.
2. He finds the weather _____.
3. She's expecting her vacation to be _____.
4. She thinks white is _____.

happy	sad
exciting	depressing
cheerful	boring
calm	disgusting

B Write your <u>own</u> response.

1. "I'm feeling really down in the dumps."
   (YOU) _____.

2. "Anything I can do?"
   (YOU) _____.

3. "She's tired of the same old grind."
   (YOU) _____.

4. "What's wrong?"
   (YOU) _____.

🎧 *TOP NOTCH* SONG
"The Colors of Love"
Lyrics on last book page.

TOP NOTCH PROJECT
Make a list of well-known
people you consider very
successful. Find information
about the size of their families
and where each person was
in the birth order of his or her
family.

TOP NOTCH WEBSITE
For Unit 7 online activities,
visit the *Top Notch*
Companion Website at
www.longman.com/topnotch.

C Complete each statement with the correct preposition.

Extroverts don't worry_____ talking in public. They believe _____
_{1.}   _{2.}
being honest, and they get bored _____ being alone. They may
_{3.}
talk _____ staying home and reading a book, but when they do,
_{4.}
they complain _____ having no one to talk to. They object _____
_{5.}   _{6.}
being by themselves.

about
in
to
with

D Complete each statement. Choose the best answer.

1. John is such an (extrovert / introvert). He loves being around other people.
2. Our usual pattern of behavior is our (genetics / personality).
3. Another word for characteristics is (nurture / traits).
4. Many people believe that (self-criticism / birth order) affects personality development.
5. The nature-nurture controversy is an argument about the origin of the (environment / personality).

E WRITING. **Write about the personality of a person you know well. Include some or all of the following words and expressions in your description.**

- self-critical
- creative
- an introvert
- a rebel
- conservative
- an extrovert
- a clown

UNIT WRAP-UP

- **Narration.** Tell a story, using the pictures.
- **Social language.** Create conversations for the wife and husband.
- **Writing.** Write about the family at the beach. Describe the personalities of the children.

Now I can ...

- ☐ discuss color preferences.
- ☐ cheer someone up.
- ☐ determine my personality type.
- ☐ discuss the impact of birth order on personality.

85

Enjoying the Arts

UNIT GOALS

1 Recommend a museum
2 Describe an object
3 Talk about how art fits in your life
4 Discuss your favorite artists

A **TOPIC PREVIEW.** Which of these pieces of art have you seen before? Are you familiar with the artists?

The Great Wave of Kanagawa / print (woodcut)
artist: Katsushika Hokusai, Japan (around 1830)

Dutch Interior I / oil painting
artist: Joan Miró, Spain (1928)

36 1/8" x 28 3/4". Mrs. Simon Guggenheim Fund.
(163.1945). ©2004 Successio Miro/Artist Rights
Society ARS, NY. The Museum of Modern Art/
Licensed by Scala-Art Resource, NY.

White Flower on Red Earth, #1 / oil painting
artist: Georgia O'Keeffe, U.S.A. (1943)

The Grinder / oil painting
artist: Diego Rivera, Mexico (1926)

Rivera, Diego (1866-1957). The Grinder (La molendera).
1926. Oil on cavas, 35 7/16 x 46 1/16 in. Museo Nacional de
Arte Moderno, Instituto Nacional de Bellas Artes, Mexico City,
D.F., Mexico. (c) Banco de Mexico Diego Rivera & Frida Kahlo
Museums Trust. Av. Cinco de Mayo No. 2, Col. Centro, Del.
Cuauhtemoc 06059, Mexico, D.F. Reproduction authorized by
the Instituto Nacional de Bellas Artes y Literatura. Courtesy of
Art Resource. NY.

B Which of these pieces of art do you like the best? Why?

> ❝ I love the Georgia O'Keeffe.
> I love nature, and the colors of the
> painting are very exciting. ❞

C 🎧 **SOUND BITES.** Read along silently as you listen to a natural conversation.

JOE: This print's sort of interesting. It says it was painted in 1903. I kind of like it.
EMMA: Is it a Picasso?
JOE: Yes, it is. It would look nice over my desk.
EMMA: Don't you find it a little too dark?
JOE: No. I think it's just right.

EMMA: Hey, what about this Warhol? What do you think?
JOE: I don't know. I'm not really too crazy about his stuff.
EMMA: Just look at the colors!
JOE: I guess I'm not into really bright colors. I prefer the Picasso.
EMMA: To each his own.

D Classify the statements. Check the ones that indicate likes. Write an "**X**" for the ones that indicate dislikes.

☐ **1.** This print's sort of interesting.
☐ **2.** I kind of like it.
☐ **3.** Don't you find it a little too dark?

☐ **4.** I think it's just right.
☐ **5.** I'm not really too crazy about his stuff.
☐ **6.** I'm not into really bright colors.

WHAT ABOUT **YOU?**

What kinds of art do you prefer?

 ☐ painting

 ☐ drawing

 ☐ photography

 ☐ sculpture

 ☐ fashion

 ☐ film

 ☐ pottery

☐ other _____

Recommend a Museum

🎧 CONVERSATION **MODEL** **Read and listen.**

A: Be sure not to miss the Prado Museum while you're in Madrid.

B: Really? Why's that?

A: Well, for one thing, *Las Meninas* is kept there.

B: No kidding! I've always wanted to see that.

A: They have a great collection of paintings. You'll love it.

B: Thanks for the suggestion!

🎧 **Rhythm and intonation practice**

Las Meninas,
by Diego Velázquez

A **GRAMMAR.** **The passive voice**

The focus of a sentence is different in the active voice and the passive voice.

Active voice: Picasso **painted** *Guernica* in 1937.
Passive voice: *Guernica* **was painted by** Picasso in 1937.

Form the passive voice with a form of <u>be</u> and the past participle of a verb.

	<u>be</u>	**past participle**	
These vases	**were**	**made**	in the sixteenth century.
The *Mona Lisa*	**is**	**kept**	at the Louvre in Paris.

> Use a **<u>by</u>** phrase to identify who performed an action.
>
> This dress was designed by Donatella Versace.

GRAMMAR BOOSTER

PAGES G15–G16
For more …

B **Change these sentences from the active to the passive voice.**

1. Leonardo da Vinci made this drawing.
   <u>This drawing was made by Leonardo da Vinci</u>.

2. Imogen Cunningham took that photograph in 1903.
   _____.

3. Vincent Van Gogh painted *The Starry Night* in 1889.
   _____.

4. Federico Fellini directed the film *La Strada* in 1954.
   _____.

5. Katsushika Hokusai made that print over a century ago.
   _____.

C 🎧 **PRONUNCIATION.** Emphatic stress. Emphasize primary stress syllables to show enthusiasm. Listen and repeat.

1. No **KIDD**ing!
2. You'll **LOVE** it!
3. That's **PER**fect!
4. How **IN**teresting!

CONVERSATION
PAIR WORK

Recommend a museum. Use the guide and the pictures, or create a new conversation about museums you know.

A: Be sure not to miss _____ while you're in _____.
B: Really? Why's that?
A: Well, for one thing, _____ is kept there.
B: _____.
A: They have a great collection of _____.
B: _____.

The National Palace Museum / Taipei, Taiwan

Known for its huge collection of Chinese painting, pottery, sculpture, and crafts.

Travelers Among Mountains and Streams, by Fan K'uan

David, by Michelangelo

The Accademia Gallery / Florence, Italy

Six million visitors a year! Famous for its collection of sculptures by Michelangelo!

The Louvre Museum / Paris, France

The world's largest art museum! And some of the world's greatest art!

Mona Lisa, by Leonardo da Vinci

CONTROLLED PRACTICE

2 *Describe an Object*

🎧 CONVERSATION MODEL Read and listen.

A: Excuse me. What's this figure made of?

B: Wood. It's handmade.

A: Really? Where was it made?

B: Mexico. What do you think of it?

A: It's fantastic.

🎧 **Rhythm and intonation practice**

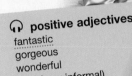

🎧 **positive adjectives**
fantastic
gorgeous
wonderful
cool (very informal)

A 🎧 VOCABULARY. Materials. Listen and practice.

| glass | silver | gold | clay | wood | stone | cloth |

B PAIR WORK. Point to one of the objects. Ask and answer questions about materials.

❝What's the English chair made of?❞

❝It's made of wood.❞

▲ an English chair

▲ an Egyptian figure

▲ an Italian vase

▲ a Japanese figure

▲ a Mexican bowl

▲ a Spanish bag

C GRAMMAR. The passive voice: questions

Yes / no questions

Were these wood bowls **made** in Africa?   Yes, they were. / No, they weren't.

Was this stone figure **carved** by the Incas?   Yes, it was. / No, it wasn't.

Information questions

Where **were** these cloth figures **made**?   In Brazil.

When **was** this picture **painted**?   It was painted in the 1960s.

What **are** these clay bowls **used** for?   They're used for cooking.

How **was** it **made**?   All by hand.

GRAMMAR BOOSTER

PAGE G17
For more …

D Unscramble the words to write questions.

1. were / Where / carved / those / wood figures _____?

2. made / were / those /dolls / How _____?

3. Was / painted / that / clay bowl / by hand _____?

4. was / taken / When / that / photograph _____?

E Write an information question for each statement.

1. _How were the glass figures made_ ?   The glass figures were made by hand.

2. _____?   The pottery is used for carrying water.

3. _____?   The gold figure was made hundreds of years ago.

4. _____?   The wood chairs were built in Venezuela.

5. _____?   The bowl was made by machine.

CONVERSATION PAIR WORK

Discuss the art objects. Use the guide, or create a new conversation.

A: What _____ made of?

B: _____.

A: Really? Where _____ made?

B: _____. What do you think of _____?

A: _____ …

Continue the conversation in your own way.

☺ It's / They're { fantastic. / gorgeous. / wonderful. / cool.

☹ I'm not crazy about / I don't care for { it. / them.
It's / They're { not for me.

▲ dolls from Guatemala

◀ a figure from New Zealand

◀ a vase from Korea

◀ a figure from Peru

◀ a vase from France

◀ a figure from Peru

CONTROLLED PRACTICE

3 ▶ *Talk about How Art Fits in Your Life*

Ⓐ READING WARM-UP. Is art an important part of your life?
Do you think artistic talent is genetic?

Ⓑ 🎧 READING. *Top Notch* interviewed two people about the role of art in their lives.

LIVING WITH ART

In 1982, Lynn Contrucci bought a beautiful piece of jewelry from Mali, in West Africa. She liked the piece so much that she began to study African art in order to understand it better. She was selling her house at the time, and she had some money to spend—so she started to collect African art. Since then, it has become a passion. She has collected nearly 300 pieces, including figures and masks. "I'm an addict now! My family thinks I'm crazy," she jokes. Even her windows and bed are decorated with beautiful African cloth. Some pieces are given as gifts to family and friends, or they are sold just to make room for more. In 1998, she began to get interested in Chinese jade figures and Tibetan paintings. More recently, she began collecting Haitian paintings. "My home is a mixture of art from all these places," she says.

Ms. Contrucci says it is like bringing people into her home. "Each piece has a special meaning. They are my friends."

Yu Gan is an artist from a family of talented artists. He began painting at the age of seven and never stopped. His father, Yu Heng, is known internationally for his dramatic traditional paintings, calligraphy, and poetry. His brother, Yu Ping, is a sculptor and painter. His sister, Yu Fan, is both a pianist and an artist. His wife, Yan Liu, is a fashion design artist, and his son, Kuai—who has shown strong artistic talent since the age of three—wants to be a filmmaker.

Mr. Yu paints in an abstract style that combines, as he puts it, "the best traditions of Western and Eastern art." Like traditional Chinese artists, he is inspired by images from nature—earth and water.

Yu Gan's son, Kuai (above)

Yu Gan's father, (left)

Like Western artists, he works with oil paint to express his feelings. He hopes to influence young Chinese with his art. "Today, they turn away from all things Chinese and love all things Western. I want them to understand that they can take the best from both worlds." Mr. Yu has a website at www.eChinaArt.com, which was created to promote art by Chinese artists worldwide.

"I am totally captivated by art," says Mr. Yu. "I can't imagine life without it."

SOURCE: Authentic *Top Notch* interviews

1. Why does Lynn Contrucci's family think she's crazy? Do <u>you</u> think she is?

2. What does Yu Gan mean when he says, "I am totally captivated by art"? Are <u>you</u>?

3. Which best describes you? Explain your answer.

    a. I collect art.   **b.** I make art.   **c.** I appreciate art.   **d.** I don't care about art.

TOP NOTCH
INTERACTION • *Is art important in your life?*

STEP 1. PAIR WORK. Answer the questions with a partner. Explain each answer.

    1. Do you or does anyone in your family have artistic talent?

    2. Do you have any friends with artistic talent?

    3. How often do you visit art museums or galleries?

    4. Do you decorate your home with art objects?

STEP 2. On your notepad, write notes about some art that decorates your home.

piece	notes
wood figure	made in Santos/small, has bright colors/helps me remember my vacation

piece	notes

STEP 3. GROUP WORK. Tell your class about the art that decorates your home. Use your notepad for support.

NEED HELP? **Here's language you already know:**

Questions

What [is it] used for?
Where [are they] from?
When [was it] made?
How [were they] made?

Likes and dislikes

I'm into ____.
I'm crazy about ____.
I don't care for____.
I can't stand ____.
I prefer ____.

Descriptions

[They're] called ["worry beads"].
[It's] made of [wood].
[They were] made by [children].

4 Discuss Your Favorite Artists

A 🎧 **VOCABULARY.** How to describe influences. **Listen and practice.**

be inspired by	She **is inspired by** nature. She tries to copy nature's beauty in her paintings.
be influenced by	He **was influenced by** the Mexican muralist Diego Rivera's art. Their paintings often have the same themes.
be interested in	He **has** always **been interested in** men's fashion. He reads about the newest designs in magazines.
be fascinated by	She**'s fascinated by** the films of Ingmar Bergman, the Swedish director. She watches them again and again.
be moved by	She **is** really **moved by** Sebastião Salgado's photographs. His images of children sometimes make her cry.

B **WHAT ABOUT YOU?** What are you interested in? Inspired by? Fascinated by?

C 🎧 **LISTENING COMPREHENSION.** Listen to the biography of Vincent Van Gogh. In your opinion, did he have an interesting life? Listen again and check T (**true**) or F (**false**).

PART 1

T F

☐ ☐ **1.** Van Gogh studied art as a child.

☐ ☐ **2.** In Paris, Van Gogh was influenced by the work of other artists.

☐ ☐ **3.** Van Gogh didn't care for Japanese art.

PART 2

T F

☐ ☐ **4.** In Arles, Van Gogh was inspired by the colors of the French countryside.

☐ ☐ **5.** Before Van Gogh died, his brother came from Paris to be with him.

☐ ☐ **6.** Many of his paintings were sold when he lived in Arles.

Zundert—the small village in Holland where Van Gogh was born

Self-portrait with Cut-off Ear and Bandage, by Van Gogh

The town of Arles in southern France

Vase with Fourteen Sunflowers, by Van Gogh

INTERACTION • *I'm really into Picasso!*

STEP 1. Look at some famous artists. Add your <u>own</u> favorites. Then write notes about your favorite artists on the notepad.

Auguste René Rodin,
sculptor (France)

Ang Lee,
director (Taiwan)

Donatella Versace,
designer (Italy)

Sebastião Salgado,
photographer (Brazil)

Mary Cassatt,
painter (USA)

Frank Gehry,
architect (Canada)

Your
favorite artists

	artist's name	type of artist	I like this artist because ...
1.			
2.			
3.			

STEP 2. GROUP WORK. Discuss your favorite artists. Tell your class why you like them.

❝I'm a real fan of Frida Kahlo and Diego Rivera. I'm fascinated by their lives.❞

❝Donatella Versace is my favorite designer. Her fashions are so contemporary!❞

❝I love Ang Lee. His films are very interesting. My favorite is *Crouching Tiger, Hidden Dragon.*❞

FREE PRACTICE

95

A 🎧 **LISTENING COMPREHENSION. Listen to the conversations. Write the letter of the piece of art they are talking about.**

1. _____ 2. _____ 3. _____ 4. _____

B Change these sentences from the active to the passive voice.

1. Akira Kurosawa directed *The Hidden Fortress*.

_____.

2. Henri Matisse made the print *Icarus* in 1947.

_____.

3. Cesar Pelli designed the Petronas Towers in Kuala Lumpur.

_____.

4. Ansel Adams took that photograph of Boulder Dam in 1942.

_____.

5. Auguste Rodin made *The Thinker* in 1880.

_____.

C Add materials to the lists. Explain your answers.

materials that can break easily	materials that are heavy	materials that are expensive
glass	_____	_____
_____	_____	_____
_____	_____	_____

D Complete the statements.

1. The art of designing clothes is called _____.
2. The art of taking pictures with a camera is called _____.
3. The art of carving figures from wood or other materials is called _____.
4. Pottery is usally made of _____.
5. A lot of jewelry is made of _____ or _____.

E **WRITING. On a separate sheet of paper, write about a piece of art that you like in your home or at a museum. What does it look like? How does it make you feel? Is it important to you? Why?**

🎧 *TOP NOTCH* SONG
"To Each His Own"
Lyrics on last book page.

TOP NOTCH PROJECT
Research information on the life of an artist you like. Write a short biography.

TOP NOTCH WEBSITE
For Unit 8 online activities, visit the *Top Notch* Companion Website at www.longman.com/topnotch.

UNIT WRAP-UP

- **Discussion.** Talk about the pieces of art you like, and why.
- **Grammar.** Make statements in the passive voice about the art.
- **Social language.** Create conversations for the people.

THE GREAT MUSEUMS OF LONDON

THE NATIONAL GALLERY

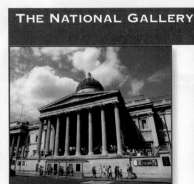

One of the greatest collections of European paintings in the world.

The Arnolfini Marriage, by Jan van Eyck (1434)

THE VICTORIA AND ALBERT MUSEUM

The Luck of Edenhall, Syria, 13th century

The greatest museum of decorative art in the world. A permanent collection of fashion, sculpture, ceramics, glass, silver and jewelry, furniture, photography, and paintings.

THE TATE GALLERY

Mustard on White, by Roy Lichtenstein (1963)

The best of British art and a major new gallery of modern art.

THE BRITISH MUSEUM

Best known for its exhibits of art from ancient Egypt, Greece, and Rome.

Discus thrower, Rome, 5th century B.C.E.

✓ Now I can ...

- ☐ recommend a museum.
- ☐ describe an object.
- ☐ talk about how art fits in my life.
- ☐ discuss my favorite artists.

Living with Computers

Unit Goals

1 Recommend a better deal
2 Troubleshoot a problem
3 Describe how you use computers
4 Discuss the social impact of the Internet

A **TOPIC PREVIEW.** Look at the electronics store website. Which of these computer accessories do you already have? Which would you like to have?

allthecoolstuff.com
WHAT THE FUTURE HAS IN STORE FOR YOU!

Shop by Departments
Weekly Specials
Computers
Computer Accessories
Software
Photo
Video
Audio
Appliances
Entertainment

HOME | my order | account | login | view cart | SEARCH [   ] GO

CHECK OUT OUR NEW MODELS!

monitors

microphones and headsets

speakers

CD drives

NEED A NEW MOUSE? CHECK OUT OUR PRICES!

keyboards and mice

NEW GAMES AVAILABLE

TRITRYST

CHESSMASTER 8000

games and joysticks

CHECK OUT OUR NEW UPDATES!

Adobe Acrobat 5.0

Adobe GoLive 4.0

Microsoft Windows NT Server

software

B **DISCUSSION.** Where do <u>you</u> get the latest information on computer and other electronics products? What are the advantages of shopping for these products online?

C 🎧 **SOUND BITES.** Read along silently as you listen to an instant message "conversation."

ron22: Hey, Deb. Are you there?
dpike: Hi, Ron. I'm surfing the net. Just log on?
ron22: Yup. Am I interrupting you?
dpike: Not at all. Just fooling around. What are you up to?
ron22: I logged on to send you some pictures.
dpike: Great! What of?
ron22: Photos of my trip!!!
dpike: Cool! Can't wait to download them.

B I U A A A A A ♪ ♥ SEND

a few minutes later ...

dpike: Hi Ron, still there?
ron22: Still here. Just deleting junk mail. Get the pix?
dpike: Yes. They took FOREVER to download!
ron22: Sorry about that.
dpike: It's OK. They're awesome. :-)
ron22: I knew you'd like them. Gotta go! Later!
dpike: See ya.

B I U A A A A A ♪ ♥ SEND

D Deb and Ron shortened sentences in their instant messages. Complete their statements with the words in the box.

| I'm Did you I See you They're Are you |

1. "_____ just log on?"
2. "_____ just fooling around."
3. "_____ photos of my trip!!!"

4. "_____ can't wait to download them."
5. "_____ still there?"
6. "_____ later!"

WHAT ABOUT **YOU?**

Check yes, no, or not sure.

Do you know what to do if:	yes	no	not sure
1. you get an instant message?	☐	☐	☐
2. your printer won't print?	☐	☐	☐
3. you can't get on the Internet?	☐	☐	☐
4. your computer crashes?	☐	☐	☐

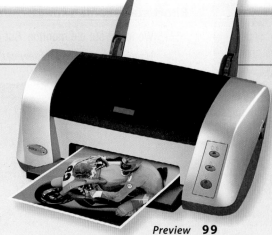

Recommend a Better Deal

🎧 CONVERSATION
MODEL Read and listen.

A: I'm thinking about getting a new monitor.

B: Oh, yeah? What kind?

A: Everyone says I should get a Macro.

B: Well, I've heard that the Panatel is as good as the Macro, but it costs a lot less.

A: Really? I'll check it out.

🎧 **Rhythm and intonation practice**

Ⓐ GRAMMAR. Comparisons with <u>as</u> ... <u>as</u>

Similarity

Use <u>as</u> ... <u>as</u> to say that two things are equal or the same.
Use the adverb <u>just</u> for emphasis.

> The F30 has **as many new features as** the LX.
> The new monitor is **just as good as** the old one.

Use the adverb <u>almost</u> to say two things are very similar, but not exactly the same.

> The X20 is **almost as good as** the X15. But it's a little slower.

Difference

Use <u>not as</u> ... <u>as</u> to say that two things are different.
Use the adverb <u>quite</u> when the difference is very small.

> My new air conditioner is**n't as noisy as** the old one.
> The F30 does**n't** cost **quite as much as** the LX.

Use the adverb <u>nearly</u> to say that there's a big difference.

> Our old monitor was**n't nearly as big as** the new one. The new one is much bigger.

Short statements with <u>as</u>

> We loved our old monitor. But our new monitor is **just as good.**
> Have you seen Carol's new car? My car is**n't nearly as nice.**

GRAMMAR BOOSTER

PAGES G17–G18
For more ...

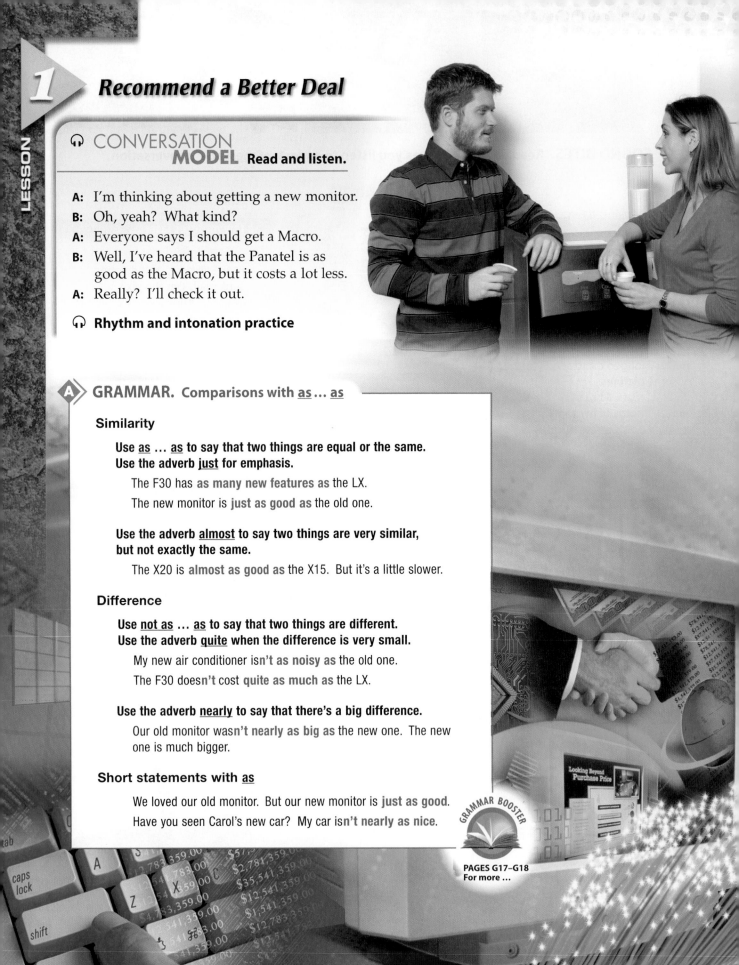

B **Read the statements. Write sentences with as … as. Use the adverbs.**

1. The Macro computer game is easy to use. The Spartica computer game is also easy to use.

   (just) _____.

2. The new RCO keyboard is popular. The one from Digitek is popular too.

   (just) _____.

3. The C50 monitor is large. The C30 monitor is a little larger than the C50 monitor.

   (almost) _____.

4. Hampton's new laptop has many new features. Jackson's new laptop also has many new features.

   (just) _____.

5. The PBS speakers are powerful. The CCV speakers are much more powerful.

   (not / nearly) _____.

6. The Panex digital camera costs US$330. The RDP digital camera costs US$360.

   (not / quite) _____.

C 🎧 **PRONUNCIATION.** Stress in as … as phrases. **Listen and repeat.**

1. The new laptop is as fast as the old one.

2. The old monitor was just as large as the new one.

3. My new keyboard isn't nearly as nice as the old one.

CONVERSATION
PAIR WORK

Student A: choose a product from *Buyer's Friend Magazine.*
Student B: recommend a better deal from *Electronics Guide Magazine.*

Use the guide, or create a new conversation.

A: I'm thinking about getting a new _____.

B: _____? What kind?

A: Everyone says I should get a _____.

B: Well, I've heard that the _____.

A: Really? I'll check it out.

BUYER'S FRIEND *Magazine*

Our recommendations!

■ Mott Optical Mouse	very good	US$25
■ Mott X16 Keyboard	very comfortable	US$19
■ Mott Super Web Camera	easy to use	US$256
■ Mott Z30 Monitor	17 inches	US$260

Electronics GUIDE magazine — YOUR BEST BUYS!

Rico PF Mouse	very good	US$20
Rico P30 Keyboard	very comfortable	US$15
Rico Ultra Web Camera	easy to use	US$200
Rico PH1 Monitor	20 inches	US$260

2 Troubleshoot a Problem

🎧 CONVERSATION MODEL **Read and listen.**

A: Eugene, could you take a look at this?

B: Sure. What's the problem?

A: Well, I clicked on the toolbar to save a file and the computer crashed.

B: Why don't you try restarting? That sometimes works.

A: OK. I'll give that a try.

🎧 **Rhythm and intonation practice**

A 🎧 **VOCABULARY.** Computer commands. **Listen and practice.**

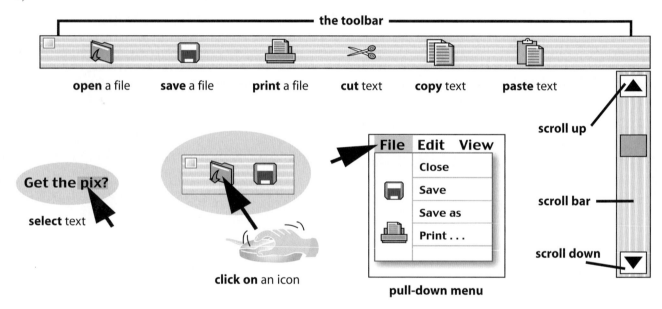

B 🎧 **LISTENING COMPREHENSION.** Listen carefully and check the command(s) the person wants to use.

1. □	□	□	□	□	□	□
2. □	□	□	□	□	□	□
3. □	□	□	□	□	□	□
4. □	□	□	□	□	□	□
5. □	□	□	□	□	□	□
6. □	□	□	□	□	□	□

The following two sentences have the same meaning.

I scrolled down **to read** the text. = I scrolled down **because I wanted to read** the text.

Use an infinitive to express a purpose.

I put the cursor on the pull-down menu **to close** the file.

Put the cursor on the toolbar **to choose** a command.

You can use short answers with infinitives to answer questions about purpose.

Why did you click on that icon?   **To save** the file before I close it.

Why did you click on that word?   **To select** it so I can copy it.

GRAMMAR BOOSTER

PAGES G18–G19
For more ...

 PAIR WORK. Look at Pat's To-Do List. Ask and answer questions. Use the infinitive of purpose.

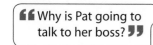

❝Why is Pat going to talk to her boss?❞ ❝To ask for a vacation day.❞

Complete each sentence in your own way. Use infinitives of purpose.

1. You can click on the print icon…

2. Put the cursor on the pull-down menu…

3. I bought a new scanner…

4. I e-mailed my friend…

5. I logged on to the Internet…

TO-DO

talk to boss—ask for a vacation day

go to supermarket—buy chicken for lunch with Mom

call Mom—invite her for lunch

take car to garage—get an oil change

meet John—help him shop for a new suit

CONVERSATION **PAIR WORK**

Ask for help with a computer problem. Use the guide, or create a new conversation.

A: _____, could you take a look at this?

B: Sure. _____?

A: Well, I _____ and _____.

B: Why don't you _____?

A: _____ …

Continue the conversation in your own way.

💡 **Some ideas…**

- The computer crashed.
- The printer won't print.
- The file won't open.
- your own idea

Describe How You Use Computers

A 🎧 **VOCABULARY.** Things to do on the Internet. **Listen and practice.**

1. surf the Internet

2. join a chat room

4. scan pictures

3. send an attachment

5. create a web page

B 🎧 **LISTENING COMPREHENSION.** Listen to the people talk about how they use their computers. **Check each person's activities.**

	Dave Grant	Cecilia Rivas	Michael Teoh	Isabelle Dewar
surfs the Internet	☐	☐	☐	☐
sends instant messages	☐	☐	☐	☐
scans pictures	☐	☐	☐	☐
downloads files	☐	☐	☐	☐
has joined a chat room	☐	☐	☐	☐
has created a website	☐	☐	☐	☐
has sent an attachment	☐	☐	☐	☐

INTERACTION • *Are you a computer addict?*

STEP 1. Complete the consumer information card about your <u>own</u> computer use.

1. I use a computer ☐ for work. ☐ for fun.
☐ for study. ☐ I never use a computer.

2. I use a computer ☐ to surf the Internet. ☐ to send e-mail.
☐ to send instant messages. ☐ to write reports.
☐ to keep in touch with people. ☐ to join chat rooms.
☐ to download music files. ☐ to download pictures.
☐ to create websites. ☐ other _____

3. I spend _____ **hours a week on a computer.**
☐ 0–10   ☐ 11–20   ☐ 21–30   ☐ 31–40   ☐ 41–50   ☐ over 50

4. Compared to other people I know,
☐ I don't spend nearly as much time on a computer as they do.
☐ I spend just as much time on a computer as they do.
☐ I spend WAY too much time on a computer.
☐ you could say I'm a computer addict.

5. ☐ **People come to me for help when they have computer trouble. They consider me an expert.**

FIRST CLASS MAIL
NO POSTAGE
NECESSARY

STEP 2. GROUP WORK. Walk around your classroom and ask your classmates questions. Write their names on the chart.

Find someone who . . .	Name
1. is a computer expert.	
2. is a computer addict.	
3. is afraid of computers.	
4. uses the Internet to meet new people.	
5. uses the Internet to avoid people.	

STEP 3. Tell your class about your classmates and how they use the computer.

4 Discuss the Social Impact of the Internet

A ▶ **READING WARM-UP.** What kinds of problems have you had with the Internet? What kinds of problems with the Internet have you heard about on the news?

B ▶ 🎧 **READING.** Read the articles about some serious problems with the Internet. Which do you think is the most serious?

China Computers Face Virus Epidemic

Four out of five computers in China, the world's largest computer and Internet market, have been affected by computer viruses, according to a report in the official state news service, China Daily. "Only 16 percent of computer users reported they were free from any viruses in their computers," reports researcher, Zhang Jian. Viruses sent through the Internet are destroying information and causing too many computers to crash, the China Daily said.

SOURCE: cnn.com

Another Hacker Hits Microsoft

One week after Microsoft reported that a hacker had gotten into its computer networks, another hacker said he entered the company's web servers on Friday. The hacker, using the name Dimitri, logged on to several of Microsoft's web servers and downloaded files containing confidential company information. A Microsoft spokesperson said, "There is always a possibility that hackers can get into a company's computer network.... There are bad people out there who will try to do bad things."

SOURCE: archive.infoworld.com

Internet Fraud Grows Worldwide

You can buy almost anything online. But did you know you could use the Internet to buy stolen credit card numbers? Internet fraud is a growing international problem. There are people out there who will buy your credit card numbers to purchase things online and have them sent to their homes. "We have people on staff constantly watching this kind of activity all over the world," said Jeff King of CyberSource, a company that manages online billing. "It definitely keeps you very busy."

SOURCE: internetnews.com

Police Look for Internet Predator

Carla White was a popular 13-year-old and a good student. But she was also meeting strangers on the Internet. Last May, Carla was found strangled to death, and police believe she met her killer online. "I can't believe she's dead," said one of her classmates. "How could anyone do this to her?" Police chief Martin Beck warns, "Parents need to know that when their children visit chat rooms, there are Internet predators out there who may want to hurt them."

SOURCE: usatoday.com

C Based on the articles, predict the person who would make each of these statements. Explain your answer.

_____ **1.** "Kids should be very careful on the Internet. It's very scary."

_____ **2.** "Our company needs better ways to protect our files from people outside."

_____ **3.** "It's costing our company a lot of time and money to make sure customers are billed correctly."

_____ **4.** "There are still too many computers in this country that may crash."

a. Martin Beck, police chief

b. Zhang Jian, researcher

c. Jeff King, CyberSource

d. A Microsoft spokesperson

TOP NOTCH
INTERACTION • _Life in cyberspace_

STEP 1. **Read the beginning of an article about the social impact of the Internet.**

> Computers have changed people's lives, and in most cases for the better. However, you have to balance the benefits with the problems—for every benefit there is also a bad side. On the good side, information is available to everyone quickly and easily through the Internet. On the bad side, not all information you find on the Internet is true. You have to check carefully before you can believe all that you read.

STEP 2. **PAIR WORK.** **Discuss some of the benefits and problems of computers and the Internet. Talk about your own experiences and things you have heard or read about in the news. Make a list of them on your notepad.**

Benefits	Problems
You can meet new people online.	Bad people use the Internet, too.

Benefits	Problems

STEP 3. **GROUP WORK.** **Discuss the benefits and problems of computers and the Internet. Compare notes and write a list of benefits and problems on the board.**

STEP 4. **WRITING.** Write a short article about the social impact of computers and the Internet. Include information about the benefits and problems.

CHECKPOINT

A 🎧 **LISTENING COMPREHENSION. Listen to the conversations. Choose the words that best describe each product. Then listen again to check your answers.**

1. The C40 Monitor is _____ the Z8 Monitor.
   a. the same as   **b.** larger than   **c.** smaller than

2. The Hip Web Camera is _____ the Pentac Web Camera.
   a. the same as   **b.** cheaper than   **c.** more expensive than

3. Mundite's new CD drive is _____ Mundite's old CD drive.
   a. the same as   **b.** faster than   **c.** slower than

4. Play Zone's computer game is _____ New World's game.
   a. the same as   **b.** less fun than   **c.** more fun than

B **Write a response to each statement in your own way.**

1. "Gotta go! Later!"
   YOU _____.

2. "I'm thinking about getting a new computer."
   YOU _____.

3. "I clicked on save and my computer crashed."
   YOU _____.

C **Answer each question in your own way, using an infinitive of purpose.**

1. Why do people join chat rooms? _____.

2. Why do people e-mail their friends? _____.

3. Why do people surf the Internet? _____.

4. Why do people visit electronics store websites? _____.

5. Why are you studying English? _____.

D **Complete the following statements.**

1. If you want to print a document, click on the print _____.

2. To read more text on your screen, use the scroll _____ to scroll down.

3. If you want to see what other things you can do, click on the _____ menu.

4. When you're finished working on a document, don't forget to _____ it before you close the file.

> **TOP NOTCH PROJECT**
> Find articles in your local newspapers and magazines about computer or Internet benefits or problems. Tell your class about them.

> **TOP NOTCH WEBSITE**
> For Unit 9 online activities, visit the *Top Notch* Companion Website at www.longman.com/topnotch.

E **WRITING. Write about how you use a computer. Talk about how often you use it and what you do with it. Or write about someone you know who uses a computer.**

UNIT WRAP-UP

- **Vocabulary.** Name the computer parts and accessories.
- **Grammar.** Write statements using the infinitive of purpose.
- **Social language.** Create conversations for the people.

✓ **Now I can ...**

- ☐ recommend a better deal.
- ☐ troubleshoot a problem.
- ☐ describe how people use computers.
- ☐ discuss the social impact of the Internet.

Ethics and Values

UNIT GOALS

1 Return someone else's property
2 Discuss ethical choices
3 Express personal values
4 Discuss honesty

A **TOPIC PREVIEW.** Study the situations. What do you think each person should do?

What should he do?

This box has the wrong price.

What should she do?

Uh-oh. Someone forgot that watch.

What should she do?

I think this total is wrong.

Guest Check

TABLE NO.	NO. PERSONS	SERVER NO.		CHECK NO. 2651
1	shrimp cocktail		9	50
1	tomato bisque		4	50
1	garden salad		6	75
1	sirloin		18	95
1	bottle sparkling water		3	00
1	espresso		2	50
	TOTAL		22	20

_ _ _ You - Call Again

GUEST RECEIPT

NO. PERSONS	DATE	CHECK NO. 2651	AMOUNT

What should he do?

But I only ordered one!

INVOICE

1 nylon windbreaker   U.S. $ 52.00

TOTAL $ 52.00

B **DISCUSSION.** Have you ever had a similar experience to any of these situations? What did you do?

C 🎧 **SOUND BITES. Read along silently as you listen to a natural conversation.**

MATT: I'm going to get a tattoo.

PAUL: Your parents would let you do that?

MATT: Are you kidding? If I asked them, they'd just say no.

PAUL: You mean you're not going to tell them?

MATT: I'd have to be nuts to ask them. But, there's nothing wrong with tattoos. Everybody has them.

PAUL: Maybe ... Matt, I hate to say this, but I think you're making a mistake. You should get permission. If you don't, I'm sure you'll be sorry.

MATT: OK. I'll give it some thought.

D **PAIR WORK. With a partner, find the answers to these questions in the conversation.**

1. What mistake does Paul think Matt is making?

2. Why won't Matt ask his parents for permission?

3. Do you agree or disagree with Paul? Explain your answer.

WHAT ABOUT **YOU?**

In your opinion, what should teenagers have to get permission for? Write yes, no, or it depends. Explain.

1. getting a tattoo:

_____

2. using makeup:

_____

3. changing hairstyles:

_____

4. face or body piercing:

_____

5. coming home late:

_____

DISCUSSION. Do teenagers and their parents usually have the same ideas about getting permission? Support your opinion with examples from real life.

Return Someone Else's Property

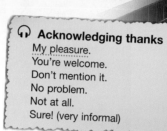

CONVERSATION MODEL Read and listen.

A: Excuse me. I think you forgot something.

B: I did?

A: Isn't this jacket hers?

B: Oh, you're right. It is. Thanks so much.

A: My pleasure.

Rhythm and intonation practice

> **Acknowledging thanks**
> My pleasure.
> You're welcome.
> Don't mention it.
> No problem.
> Not at all.
> Sure! (very informal)

A GRAMMAR. Possessive pronouns

Use possessive pronouns in place of nouns.

That coat is my coat. = That coat is **mine**.
Which coat is your coat? = Which coat is **yours**?

Don't use a noun after a possessive pronoun.

These shoes are **mine**. NOT ~~They're mine shoes.~~

subject pronouns	possessive adjectives	possessive pronouns
I	my	**mine**
you	your	**yours**
he	his	**his**
she	her	**hers**
we	our	**ours**
they	their	**theirs**

B Rewrite the following sentences. Substitute possessive pronouns for the highlighted phrases.

1. Those gloves are my gloves. *Those gloves are mine* _____.

2. That is her coat. _____.

3. The books on that table are Daniel's books. _____.

4. Their car and our car are parked on the same street. _____.

5. Are those my tickets or her tickets? _____?

6. The white house is my mother's house. _____.

7. Is this painting your painting or her brother's painting?

_____?

C **Complete the following statements and questions. Choose the right answer.**

1. **A:** Whose umbrella is this, _____ or _____?
           he / his   _her / hers_
   B: I'm not sure. Ask them if it's _____.
                                        their / theirs

2. **A:** Who is stricter? Your parents or Jerome's?

   B: _____, I think. _____ parents aren't strict at all.
         He / His   _My / Mine_

3. **A:** Is this _____ suitcase?
              ours / our
   B: No, I already have _____ suitcase, so this one can't be _____.
                             our / ours   _our / ours_

4. **A:** I found this bracelet on the bus. Is it _____?
                                                her / hers
   B: No, it's _____ bracelet. I'm so happy someone found it!
                   my / mine

5. **A:** Is that _____ car?
              their / theirs
   B: No, _____ is the black one over there.
             their / theirs

6. **A:** Where should we meet? At _____ house or _____?
                                   your / yours   _my / mine_
   B: Neither. Let's meet at _____ office.
                                 my / mine

CONVERSATION
PAIR WORK

Collect personal items to use in the pair work, or use the pictures. In pairs or groups of three, return something that belongs to someone else. Start like this:

A: Excuse me. I think you forgot something.
B: I did?
A: _____?
B: _____.

2 Discuss Ethical Choices

CONVERSATION MODEL Read and listen.

A: Look at this. They didn't charge us for the desserts.

B: Really? We'd better tell the waiter.

A: You think so?

B: Absolutely. If we didn't tell him, it would be wrong.

Rhythm and intonation practice

> **Confirming responses**
> Absolutely.
> Definitely.
> Of course.
> Sure.

A GRAMMAR. Factual and unreal conditional sentences: meaning

Factual conditionals: present

If I **eat** too much, I **gain** weight.

If you **speak** English, you **can speak** to people all over the world.

Factual conditionals: future

If I **ask** my parents for permission, they**'ll say** no.

If they **tell** me getting a tattoo is wrong, I **won't get** one.

Unreal conditionals: present

If I **spoke** Greek, I **would apply** for that job. (unreal: I don't speak Greek, so I won't apply for the job.)

If her parents **knew** about her tattoo, they **would be** angry. (unreal: They don't know, so they are not angry.)

GRAMMAR BOOSTER

PAGES G19–20
For more...

B GRAMMAR. Unreal conditional sentences: form

Use the simple past tense in the <u>if</u> clause. For the verb <u>be</u>, always use <u>were</u>. Use <u>would</u> and a base form in the result clause.

if clause (unreal condition)	result clause (unreal result)
If Paul **pierced** his ears,	his father **would be** angry.
If Marie **were** 21,	she **would pierce** her ears.

Don't use <u>would</u> in the <u>if</u> clause.

If I **found** a wallet, I would return it. NOT If I ~~would find~~ a wallet, I would return it.

> **Questions**
> Would you ask your parents if you wanted a tattoo? What would you do if you were 21?

GRAMMAR BOOSTER

PAGE G21
For more ...

C Read the following conditional sentences. Check the ones that describe an unreal condition (a condition that does not exist).

☐ **1.** If we eat in a restaurant, I'll pay the bill.

☐ **2.** If you get a haircut, you can charge it to your room.

☐ **3.** If he came home really late, his parents would worry.

☐ **4.** If I were you, I'd tell the truth.

☐ **5.** If they find valuable things on the street, they always try to find the owner.

☐ **6.** If they sent me the wrong coat, I would return it.

D Complete each unreal conditional sentence with the correct form of the verb.

1. If I _____ tickets, I _____ to the concert at the mall.
   _{have}   _{go}

2. If his father _____ angry, he _____ off the earrings.
   _{get}   _{take}

3. If the check _____ not correct, she _____ it.
   _{be}   _{not pay}

4. If they _____ the wrong package, they _____ the mail-order company.
   _{receive}   _{call}

5. If I _____ the best place to get my ears pierced, I _____ there.
   _{know}   _{go}

E 🎧 **PRONUNCIATION.** Assimilation of sounds. **Notice how /d/ + /y/ becomes /dʒ/. Listen and repeat.**

1. What would you do if you found a wallet on the street?

2. What would you do if the waiter didn't charge you for the dessert?

3. Who would you call if you were sick?

4. Where would you go if you wanted a great meal?

F 🎧 **VOCABULARY.** Some moral dilemmas. **Listen and practice.**

They didn't charge us for the cake.

They undercharged me.

They gave me too much change.

They gave me more than I ordered.

CONVERSATION
PAIR WORK

Discuss ethical choices. Use the guide and the situations, or use your <u>own</u> ideas.

A: Look. _____.
B: _____? We'd better _____.
A: You think so?
B: _____. If we _____, _____.

You see money on the floor near a man who is putting his wallet into his pocket. You are pretty sure the money fell out of his wallet.

You see an expensive suit with a mistake on the price tag. The suit should cost twice as much.

You look at the check for a restaurant meal. They didn't charge you enough.

3 Express Personal Values

LESSON

A 🎧 **LISTENING COMPREHENSION.** **Listen to the conversations.**
Check <u>true</u> (T) or <u>false</u> (F).

       T F

1. ☐ ☐ **a.** Beth thinks it's OK for Luke to wear an earring to the office.
   ☐ ☐ **b.** Luke agrees with Beth.

2. ☐ ☐ **a.** Celia's husband has a tattoo.
   ☐ ☐ **b.** Celia's husband likes Celia's tattoo.

3. ☐ ☐ **a.** His daughter married a lawyer.
   ☐ ☐ **b.** He wants his daughter to stay home and have children.

4. ☐ ☐ **a.** Kate's dad likes the way Kate is dressed.
   ☐ ☐ **b.** Kate's dad thinks girls don't have to be modest.

B **Read the following quotations from the conversations.**
Then choose the correct definition for the underlined
word or phrase. Listen again if necessary.

1. "But lots of people are <u>old-fashioned</u>, and they
   don't think men should wear earrings."
   a. have ideas from the past
   b. don't like traditions

2. "What <u>a double standard</u>!"
   a. the same rules for all people
   b. different rules for different people

3. "That's a little <u>sexist</u>, if you ask me!"
   a. the idea that men and women are not equal
   b. the idea that men and women are equal

4. "But <u>modesty</u> is very important for girls."
   a. wearing clothes that cover their bodies
   b. wearing clothes that show their bodies

C **PAIR WORK. Think of an example for each word or phrase.**
Write your ideas in the chart. Share your ideas with a partner.

> ❝A lot of people think it's
> OK for men to wear shorts,
> but not for women.❞

old-fashioned	
a double standard	
sexist	
modesty	

STEP 1. **Fill out the Values Self-Test. Then discuss with your partner.**

VALUES SELF-TEST

Check the boxes that best describe <u>your</u> values. Include a specific example.

❑ I'm modern in my attitudes about modesty.
❑ I'm old-fashioned in my attitudes about modesty.

Explain _____

_____

❑ I think tattoos and body piercing are OK for men.
❑ I think tattoos and body piercing are OK for women.

Explain _____

_____

❑ I think it's OK to have a double standard for different people.
❑ I think the rules should be the same for everyone.

Explain _____

_____

❑ Some people might say I'm sexist.
❑ Nobody would say I'm sexist.

Explain _____

_____

**STEP 2. DISCUSSION. Discuss one or more of the following questions.
Give reasons and examples.**

1. Is it sometimes OK to have a double standard
for men and women?

2. Can people be sexist when they talk about
men, or only about women?

3. Are old-fashioned ideas usually better or
worse than modern ideas?

**STEP 3. WRITING. On a separate sheet of
paper, write your ideas about modesty
and personal appearance. How should
men dress? How should women dress?**

Man measuring the length of woman's
swimsuit in the 1920s (U.S.)

FREE PRACTICE

4 Discuss Honesty

A **READING WARM-UP.** Do you know what a lost-and-found is? Is there one in your city or town? Where?

B 🎧 **READING.** Read the article about the Tokyo lost-and-found.

Tokyo Lost-and-Found
KEEPS EYE ON GOODS

TOKYO—If it can be lost on the streets of Tokyo, it can be found in the city's cavernous lost-and-found center, where everything from diamond rings to dentures and millions of dollars in stray cash await their rightful, if forgetful, owners. On any given day, about 800,000 items pack the four-story warehouse, with 5,000 new ones trucked in every morning for an annual haul of 220,000 articles of clothing, 30,000 mobile phones, 18,000 eyeglasses, and 17,000 wallets.

Everything from diamond rings to dentures ...

"I'm not surprised anymore by what people lose," says custodian Nobuo Hasuda as he walks along the paths between wheelchairs, snowshoes, motorcycle

...30,000 mobile phones, 18,000 eyeglasses, and 17,000 wallets...

helmets, and trumpets. There are file cabinets labeled "Mobile Phones: April," "Wallets: March," and "Eyeglasses: February."

Last year, about 1.62 million articles passed through the center, making it possibly the world's biggest lost-and-found. About 250 hopefuls visit each day to see if their lost keys, briefcases, and billfolds are there.

Typical of a country obsessed with order and detail, every item is scrupulously labeled with time and place of recovery, then computer archived—no matter how seemingly trivial. One Good Samaritan turned in a phone card worth only 42 cents. It's now tagged and waiting in a drawer cluttered with half-used train passes.

...wheelchairs, snowshoes, motorcycle helmets, and trumpets...

SOURCE: The Daily Mail www.dailymailnews.com

C **Answer the following questions.**

1. Have you ever found something you lost at a lost-and-found?
2. Would you take something you found to a lost-and-found?

D **PAIR WORK.** Which of these articles would <u>you</u> take to a lost-and-found? Which ones would you <u>not</u> take there? Explain your answers.

a diamond ring	a set of dentures	a cell phone
a pair of eyeglasses	a wallet	a wheelchair
a snowshoe	a trumpet	a motorcycle helmet

E **DISCUSSION.** What do most people do when they find something valuable? Do you think most people are honest?

TOP NOTCH
INTERACTION • *What would YOU do?*

STEP 1. **Look at the situations. Answer the questions on the notepads.**

Situation: You find a wallet full of cash.
What could you do?
What should you do?
What would you do?
What would most people do?

Situation: You find a gold watch in a department store dressing room.
What could you do?
What should you do?
What would you do?
What would most people do?

Situation: The cashier undercharges you.
What could you do?
What should you do?
What would you do?
What would most people do?

Situation: You find cash near an ATM.
What could you do?
What should you do?
What would you do?
What would most people do?

STEP 2. DISCUSSION. **Discuss what you wrote about each situation. Would you do what most people would do?**

> "If I found the wallet, I would call the person on the phone. It would be wrong to keep the money."

> "If I found cash near an ATM, I would keep it. There would be no way to find the owner."

UNIT 10
CHECKPOINT

A ∩ LISTENING COMPREHENSION. Listen to the conversations and check the statements that are true.

1. ☐ John doesn't think his grandmother is too old for a tattoo.
   ☐ John has a double standard.

2. ☐ Jessica and her mother are discussing Jessica's rules.
   ☐ Jessica thinks her mother is sexist.

3. ☐ Emily and Robert are discussing right and wrong.
   ☐ The waiter charged Emily and Robert too much for their dinner.

TOP NOTCH PROJECT
To help visitors understand appropriate appearance in your country, find pictures in magazines or newspapers that depict appropriate and inappropriate appearance. Make a do's and don'ts book.

TOP NOTCH WEBSITE
For Unit 10 online activities, visit the *Top Notch* Companion Website at www.longman.com/topnotch.

B Rewrite sentences with possessive pronouns.

1. Those shoes belong to my daughter.   *They're hers*_____.

2. That coat belongs to my son.   _____.

3. The house across the street is my parents' house.   _____.

4. These coins are my husband's and mine.   _____.

5. The table over there is your table.   _____.

C Complete each conditional sentence. Use your __own__ words.

1. If the weather is bad this weekend, _____.

2. If _____, I'll go out to eat tonight.

3. If I found your wallet, _____.

4. If _____, I always call home.

5. If I had a new car, _____.

D What would __you__ do? Write an unreal conditional sentence beginning with __If__.

1. You have two sandwiches for lunch, but they only charge you for one.
   If _____.

2. You pay for a newspaper that costs one dollar with a five-dollar bill.
   The merchant gives you nine dollars change.
   If _____.

3. You order a PDA from a mail-order company. You see that there are two PDAs and a cell phone in the box.
   If _____.

E WRITING. On a separate sheet of paper, write a story about a time you or someone else had to make an ethical choice.

UNIT WRAP-UP

- **Narration.** Tell a story, using the pictures.
- **Grammar.** Write what you would do in this situation.
- **Social language.** Create conversations for the people.

Now I can ...

- ☐ return someone else's property.
- ☐ discuss ethical choices.
- ☐ express personal values.
- ☐ discuss honesty.

Alphabetical word list

This is an alphabetical list of all productive vocabulary in the *Top Notch 2* units. The numbers refer to the page on which the word first appears or is defined. When a word has two meanings, both are in the list.

A
a lot of   53
accident   40
action film   18
addict   66
address people   2
afraid of   78
agree   23
air-conditioned   39
airport shuttle   27
aisle   52
allergic to   64
almost   100
already   7
always   16
angry about   78
animated film   18
any   53
anyone   54
apologize for   78
appointment   54
art exhibition   5
as   100
asparagus   65
automatic transmission   39
avoid   64

B
babysitting   27
before   7
believe in   78
bell service   27
birth order   82
blue   75
body lotion   52
bored with   78
boring   20
bow   2
bowl   90
brake   40
brand   51
bring up (a newspaper)   32
brush   52
bumper   40
business card   2
business center   31

C
calm   77
can't stand   66

CD drive   98
cell phone   118
charge   115
charming   82
cheer (someone) up   75
cheerful   77
chewy   70
chocolate   65
clay   90
click on (an icon)   102
climb   6
cloth   90
clown   82
clutch   40
comb   52
comedy   18
compact car   44
complain about   78
convertible   44
cool   90
copy text   102
cosmetic surgery   58
crash   102
crazy about   66
create a web page   104
creative   82
crunchy   70
cut off other drivers   47
cut text   102

D
damage   40
dashboard   40
definitely   66
dental floss   52
dentures (a set of)   118
deodorant   52
depressing   77
diamond ring   118
disagree   23
disgusting   77
documentary   18
don't agree with me   64
don't care for   64
door (car)   40
double room   30
double standard   116
down   75
down in the dumps   75

download   99
drama   18
drawing   87
driver's license   39
drop off   42

E
emergency brake   40
emotions   80
engine   40
environment   80
ever   7
exchange   2
excited about   78
exciting   77
extra   32
extrovert   81
eyeglasses (a pair of)   118

F
facial   56
familiar   4
fantastic   90
fascinated by   94
fashion   87
feel 23
figure   90
fill up   42
film   87
fitness center   31
flash lights   47
for   16
fries   65
full-size car   44
funny   20

G
game   98
gas pedal   40
gearshift   40
genetics   80
gesture   8
get stuck in traffic   17
gift shop   31
glass   90
go sightseeing   6
go to the top of   6
gold   90
gorgeous   90

greetings   2
gym   5

H
had better   31
hair care   50
hair spray   52
hair dryer   32
haircut   54
hanger   32
happy   77
happy about   78
hard   70
headlight   40
headset   98
hers   112
his   112
honk   47
hood   40
horn   40
horror film   18
hug   2

I
ice cream   65
icon   102
influenced by   94
inspired by   94
instant message   99
interested in   94
Internet connection   27
introvert   81
iron   32

J
join a chat room   104
joystick   98
just   16

K
keyboard   98
king-size bed   30
kiss   2

L
last name   2
late   16
lately   16
laundry   27
lifestyle   65
look (like)   70

lose weight   64
lost-and-found   118
luxury car   44

M

ma'am   40
make up the room   32
makeup   52
mango   65
manicure   54
manual transmission   39
many   53
massage   56
medicine   50
message   28
microphone   98
mine   112
minibar   27
miss (the bus)   17
modesty   116
monitor   98
motorcycle helmet   118
mouse   98
moved by   94
much   53
museum   89
musical   18

N

nail care   53
nail clipper   52
nail file   52
nature   80
nearly   100
nervous   77
noodle   65
not pay attention   41
not signal   47
not stop   47
nurture   80

O

object to   78
old-fashioned   116
on a diet   64
only   16
open a file   102
opinion   111
ours   112
out of sorts   75
owe   16

P

painting   87
parking space   17
pasta   65
paste text   102

pedicure   54
permission   111
personality   80
photocopying   27
photography   87
pick up   42
pick up the laundry   32
pool   31
pottery   87
print a file   102
pull-down menu   102

Q

queen-size bed   30
quite   100

R

razor   52
razor blade   52
rearview mirror   40
rebel   82
recently   16
reservation   39
road sign   46
rollaway bed   30
romantic   20
room service   27

S

sad   77
sad about   78
salty   70
sardine   65
sauna   31
save a file   102
scan pictures   104
science fiction film (sci-fi)   18
scissors (a pair of)   52
scroll bar   102
scroll down   102
scroll up   102
sculpture   87
seat belt   40
sedan   44
select text   102
self-critical   82
send an attachment   104
send e-mails   105
sexist   116
shake hands   2
shampoo (product)   52
shampoo (service)   54
shave   54
shaving   50
shaving cream   52
shellfish   65

shoe shine   27
shower cap   52
sibling   82
sick of   78
side-view mirror   40
signal   40
silly   20
silver   90
since   16
single room   30
sir   40
skin care   50
skirt hanger   32
small talk   2
smell (like)   70
smoking/non-smoking   30
snowshoe   118
so far   16
soap   52
soft   70
software   98
some   53
someone   54
sour   70
speaker   98
speed   41
spicy   70
sports car   44
station wagon   44
steak   65
steering wheel   40
still   16
stone   90
suite   30
sunscreen   52
surf the Internet   104
sushi   65
SUV   44
sweet   70

T

tailgate   41
taillight   40
take a tour of   6
take away the dishes   32
take pictures of   6
talk about   78
talk on a cell phone   41
taste (like)   70
tattoo   111
terrific   66
theater   5
theirs   112
thermometer   52
think   23
thoughts   80

tip   56
tire   40
tired of   78
tofu   65
tool bar   102
tooth care   50
toothbrush   52
toothpaste   52
towel   32
traffic   17
treat   16
trumpet   118
trunk   40
try   6
turn down the beds   32
turn off   42
turn on   42
twin bed   30

U

undercharge   115
unforgettable   20
used to   67

V

values   82
van   44
vase   90
vegetarian   64
violence   22
violent   20

W

wake-up service   27
wallet   118
weave through traffic   47
weird   20
wheelchair   118
why don't   65
will   28
window (car)   40
windshield   40
windshield wiper   40
wonderful   90
wood   90
worry about   78
would rather   19
wrong   111

Y

yet   7
yours   112

Social language list

This is a unit-by-unit list of all the productive social language from *Top Notch 2*.

Unit 1

You look familiar.
Have we met before?
I don't think so.
I'm not from around here.
As a matter of fact, I am.
Oh, that's right! Now I remember.

What have you been up to?
Not much.
[Audrey], have you met [Hanah]?
[Hanah], I'd like you to meet [Audrey].
I think we've met before.
Good to see you again.

Welcome to [Rio].
Have you ever been here before?
No. It's my first time.
Have you tried [feijoada] yet?
I think you'll like it.

Unit 2

You're going to love [this theater].
I'm really in the mood for [a good classic movie].
I missed it.
They say it's [great].
Actually, I'd rather see something else.
Deal!
Sorry I'm late. Have you been here long?
For about [10] minutes. Not too bad.
I got stuck in traffic.
I missed the bus.

I couldn't get a taxi.
I couldn't find a parking space.
The [8:00] show for [*The Train*] is sold out.
How much do I owe?
Nothing. It's on me.
Next time it's my treat.
I've always wanted to see [Hitchcock's *The Birds*].
What would you rather see—a [comedy] or a [musical]?
It doesn't matter to me.

What do you think of [Madonna]?
Actually, not much.
For real? (to express surprise)
That's what makes the world go 'round!
Who was in it?
What was it about?
What kind of movie was it?
Was it good?
Do you recommend it?
I agree / disagree.

Unit 3

I'm checking out.
Was your stay satisfactory?
Will you be putting this on your [Vista card]?
Thank you for staying with us.
I'd like to speak to [Anne Smith].
I'll ring that room for you.

He's / She's not answering.
Would you like to leave a message?
Please tell him [Tim Klein] called.
Please tell her I'll call back later.
Please tell him I'll be [at the Clayton Hotel] until [5:00].
Please tell her I'll be at [22-56-838]
Is that all?

I'm checking in. The name's [Smith].
How do you want to pay?
By the way, is the [restaurant] still open?
Actually, you'd better hurry.

Unit 4

I have a reservation.
We were expecting you.
I'll need to see your [driver's license and a major credit card].
That's correct.
That'll be fine.
I had an accident.
How awful.
Oh no!
I'm sorry to hear that.
I'm so sorry. Are you OK?
No one was hurt.

Thank goodness. How did it happen?
[The other driver] was [speeding].
I hit another car. / Another car hit me.
Was there much damage?
I'll only have to replace [a taillight].
Fill it up, please, with [regular].
Yes, sir / ma'am.
Anything else?
My [turn signal] isn't working. Can you fix it?
Can you drop the car off [tomorrow morning] at about [9:00]?

What time can I pick it up?
How's [noon]?
Terrific. I'll see you at [9:00].
[My headlight] won't turn on / turn off.
[My car trunk] won't open / close.
[My engine] is making a funny sound.
[My headlight] isn't working.
[My car window] is stuck.

Unit 5

I need to pick up a few things on the way back to [the hotel].
Feel like stopping at [a cosmetics store] with me?
I'd like to, but I think I'll pass.
I don't have much time today.
It'll be a piece of cake.
Where would I find [toothpaste]?
Have a look in [aisle 2].

Actually, I did and there wasn't any.
Let me get you some from the back.
I have [a two o'clock] appointment for a [haircut] with [Sean].
[Sean] is running a little late.
Can I get you some [coffee] or [tea]?
Can I get a [manicure] in the meantime?
Yes, but it'll be a few minutes.
There's someone ahead of you.

Would it be possible to get a [facial]?
I don't have an appointment.
How long will I have to wait?
How much do you charge for a [massage]?
Is it customary to leave a tip?
Can I charge it to my room?
I'm sorry. I have to cancel my appointment.

Unit 6

What in the world are you [eating]?
I used to be. Not anymore.
To tell you the truth, it was just too much trouble.
Want to try some?
You only live once.
Everything's ready. Why don't we [sit down]?
This [food] looks great!
It really smells delicious.
Please help yourself.

Thanks. But I'll pass on the [chicken].
Don't you eat [chicken]?
I'm on a diet.
I'm trying to lose weight.
I'm avoiding [sugar].
I'm a vegetarian.
I'm allergic to [chocolate].
[Coffee] doesn't agree with me.
I'm sorry. I didn't know that.
Don't worry about it. It's not a problem.

I used to have it a lot. But I've been cutting back.
I couldn't live without it.
I'm [not] crazy about [seafood].
I'm a big [meat] eater / [coffee] drinker.
I'm a [chocolate] addict / [pizza] lover.
I can't stand [fish].
I don't care for [steak].
I'm not much of a [pizza] eater / [coffee] lover.

Unit 7

What do you feel like doing after dinner?
I'm kind of down in the dumps.
You (do) look a little blue. Something wrong?
Nothing I can put my finger on.
I guess I'm just feeling a little out of sorts.

Maybe [a nice dinner] will cheer you up.
Why don't we [go for a walk]?
Would you like me to [make you some soup]?
How about some [ice cream]? That always makes me feel better.
How about [gray]? (to talk about color preference)

[Gray]'s out of the question.
What's wrong with [gray]?
You look down. What's up?
Oh, nothing serious.
I'm just tired of the same old grind.
But thanks for asking.
I know what you mean.

Unit 8

This [print]'s sort of interesting.
I kind of like it.
It would look nice [over my desk].
Don't you find it a little too [dark]?
I guess I'm not really into [bright colors].
To each his own.
Be sure not to miss [the Prado Museum] while you're in [Madrid].
Really? Why's that?

Well, for one thing, [Las Meninas] is [kept] there.
No kidding! I've always wanted to see that.
Thanks for the suggestion.
What's this [figure] made of?
Wood. It's handmade.
What is it used for?
When were they made?

How were they made?
What do you think of it?
I'm not crazy about it / them.
I don't care for it / them.
It's not for me.
They're fantastic / gorgeous / wonderful / cool.

Unit 9

Am I interrupting you?
[I'm] just fooling around.
What are you up to?
I logged on to [send you some pictures].
Cool!
[I] can't wait to [download them].

I'm thinking about getting [a new monitor].
Oh, yeah? What kind?
Everyone says I should get [a Macro].
Well, I've heard that the [Panatel] is as [good] as the [Macro].

Really? I'll check it out.
[Eugene], could you take a look at this?
Sure. What's the problem?
Why don't you try [restarting]?
OK. I'll give that a try.

Unit 10

Your parents would let you do that?
Are you kidding?
I'd have to be nuts to [ask them].
There's nothing wrong with [tattoos]. Everybody has [them].
I hate to say this, but I think you're making a mistake.
You should get permission. If you don't, I'm sure you'll be sorry.

I'll give it some thought.
Excuse me, I think you forgot something.
My pleasure.
You're welcome.
Don't mention it.
Not at all.
Sure. (to acknowledge thanks)
They didn't charge us for the [desserts].

They undercharged me.
They gave me too much change.
They gave me more than I ordered.
You think so?
Absolutely.
Definitely.
Of course.
Sure. (to express certainty)

Pronunciation table

These are the pronunciation symbols used in *Top Notch 2*.

Vowels

Symbol	Key Word	Symbol	Key Word
i	beat, feed	ə	banana, among
ɪ	bit, did	ɚ	shirt, murder
eɪ	date, paid	aɪ	bite, cry, buy, eye
ɛ	bet, bed	aʊ	about, how
æ	bat, bad	ɔɪ	voice, boy
ɑ	box, odd, father	ɪr	deer
ɔ	bought, dog	ɛr	bare
oʊ	boat, road	ɑr	bar
ʊ	book, good	ɔr	door
u	boot, food, flu	ʊr	tour
ʌ	but, mud, mother		

Consonants

Symbol	Key Word	Symbol	Key Word
p	pack, happy	z	zip, please, goes
b	back, rubber	ʃ	ship, machine, station, special, discussion
t	tie		
d	die	ʒ	measure, vision
k	came, key, quick	h	hot, who
g	game, guest	m	men
tʃ	church, nature, watch	n	sun, know, pneumonia
dʒ	judge, general, major	ŋ	sung, ringing
f	fan, photograph	w	wet, white
v	van	l	light, long
θ	thing, breath	r	right, wrong
ð	then, breathe	y	yes
s	sip, city, psychology	t̮	butter, bottle
		tʔ	button

Irregular verbs

base form	simple past	past participle	base form	simple past	past participle
be	was / were	been	leave	left	left
become	became	become	let	let	let
begin	began	begun	lose	lost	lost
break	broke	broken	make	made	made
bring	brought	brought	mean	meant	meant
build	built	built	meet	met	met
buy	bought	bought	pay	paid	paid
catch	caught	caught	put	put	put
choose	chose	chosen	quit	quit	quit
come	came	come	read /rid/	read /rɛd/	read /rɛd/
cost	cost	cost	ride	rode	ridden
cut	cut	cut	ring	rang	rung
do	did	done	rise	rose	risen
draw	drew	drawn	run	ran	run
dream	dreamed / dreamt	dreamed / dreamt	say	said	said
drink	drank	drunk	see	saw	seen
drive	drove	driven	sell	sold	sold
eat	ate	eaten	send	sent	sent
fall	fell	fallen	shake	shook	shaken
feed	fed	fed	sing	sang	sung
feel	felt	felt	sit	sat	sat
fight	fought	fought	sleep	slept	slept
find	found	found	speak	spoke	spoken
fit	fit	fit	spend	spent	spent
fly	flew	flown	stand	stood	stood
forget	forgot	forgotten	steal	stole	stolen
get	got	gotten	swim	swam	swum
give	gave	given	take	took	taken
go	went	gone	teach	taught	taught
grow	grew	grown	tell	told	told
have	had	had	think	thought	thought
hear	heard	heard	throw	threw	thrown
hit	hit	hit	understand	understood	understood
hold	held	held	wake up	woke up	woken up
hurt	hurt	hurt	wear	wore	worn
keep	kept	kept	win	won	won
know	knew	known	write	wrote	written

Verb tense review: present, past, and future

 THE PRESENT OF <u>BE</u>

Statements

I	am	
You We They	are	late.
He She It	is	

 THE SIMPLE PRESENT TENSE

Statements

I You We They	speak English.
He She	speaks English.

<u>Yes</u> / <u>no</u> questions

Do	I you we they	know them?
Does	he she	eat meat?

Short answers

Yes,	I you we they	do.	No,	I you we they	don't.
	he she it	does.		he she it	doesn't.

Information questions

What do	you we they	need?
When does	he she it	start?
Who	wants needs likes	this book?

 THE PRESENT CONTINUOUS

Statements

I	am	watching TV.
You We They	are	studying English.
He She It	is	arriving now.

<u>Yes</u> / <u>no</u> questions

Am	I	
Are	you we they	going too fast?
Is	he she it	

Short answers

Yes,	I	am.	No,	I'm not.
	you	are.		you aren't / you're not.
	he she it	is.		he isn't / he's not. she isn't / she's not. it isn't / it's not.
	we they	are.		we aren't / we're not. they aren't / they're not.

Information questions

What	are	you we they	doing?
When	is	he she it	leaving?
Where	am	I	staying tonight?
Who	is		driving?

 THE PAST OF <u>BE</u>

Statements

I He She It	was late.
We You They	were early.

(The past of be–continued)

Yes / no questions

Was	I he she it	on time?
Were	we you they	in the same class?

Short answers

Yes,	I he she it	was.
	we you they	were.

No,	I he she it	wasn't.
	we you they	weren't.

Information questions

Where	were	we? you? they?
When	was	he she it	here?
Who	were	they?
Who	was	he? she? it?

5 THE SIMPLE PAST TENSE

Many verbs are irregular in the simple past tense.
See the list of irregular verbs on page 126.

Statements

I You He She It We They	stopped working.

I You He She It We They	didn't start again.

Yes / no questions

Did	I you he she it we they	make a good dinner?

Short answers

Yes,	I you he she it we they	did.

No,	I you he she it we they	didn't.

Information questions

When did	I you he she it we they	read that?
Who		called?

6 THE FUTURE WITH BE GOING TO

Statements

I'm You're He's She's It's We're They're	going to	be here soon.

I'm You're He's She's It's We're They're	not going to	be here soon.

Yes / no questions

Are	you we they	going to want coffee?
Am	I	going to be late?
Is	he she it	going to arrive on time?

Short answers

Yes,	I	am.
	you	are.
	he she it	is.
	we they	are.

No,	I'm not. you aren't / you're not. he isn't / he's not. she isn't / she's not. it isn't / it's not. we aren't / we're not. they aren't / they're not.

Information questions

What	are	you we they	going to see?
When	is	he she it	going to shop?
Where	am	I	going to stay tomorrow?
Who	is		going to call?

GRAMMAR BOOSTER

The *Grammar Booster* is optional. It provides more explanation and practice, as well as additional grammar concepts.

UNIT 1   Lesson 1

A Complete the sentences with the present perfect or the simple past tense.

I _____ in São Paulo, Brazil all my life. However, I _____ to a lot of other
   1. live   2. be
places too. I _____ to Europe three times. In 1999, I _____ to Amsterdam,
              3. fly   4. go
Vienna, and Prague. It _____ a wonderful trip. I _____ Europe again in 2000
                        5. be   6. visit
and 2003. On that trip, I _____ the Eiffel Tower in Paris, _____ sightseeing
                           7. climb   8. go
in London, and _____ a bullfight in Madrid. Of course, I _____ all over
                9. see   10. travel
Latin America too. In 2004, I _____ the United States and Canada for the first time. I
                               11. tour
_____ to Asia, but I'd really like to go.
12. be / not

The present perfect: information questions with <u>What</u> or <u>Which</u> and a noun

Use <u>What</u> or <u>Which</u> and the present perfect to ask for information about an indefinite
time in the past.
   What (OR Which) languages **have** you **studied**?
   What (OR Which) countries **have** you **visited**?
   What (OR Which) dishes **have** you **tried**?

B Use the topics to write questions with <u>What</u> or <u>Which</u> in the present perfect.
Then write answers to the questions in your own way.

1. (big cities) *What big cities have you visited* _____?

   Answer: _____.

2. (new songs) _____?

   Answer: _____.

3. (restaurants) _____?

   Answer: _____.

4. (airlines) _____?

   Answer: _____.

5. (movies) _____?

   Answer: _____.

The present perfect: use and placement of <u>yet</u> and <u>already</u>

Use <u>yet</u> in present perfect questions and negative statements. Put <u>yet</u> at the end of the sentence.

questions	negative statements
Have you read the book **yet**?	I haven't read the book **yet**.

Use <u>already</u> in present perfect questions and affirmative statements. Put <u>already</u> before the main verb or at the end of the sentence.

questions	affirmative statements
Have you **already** read the book?	I've **already** read the book.
OR Have you read the book **already**?	OR I've read the book **already**.

BE CAREFUL!

Don't use <u>yet</u> in present perfect affirmative statements.
  DON'T SAY Yes, I've read the book ~~yet~~.

Don't use <u>already</u> in present perfect negative statements.
  DON'T SAY No, I haven't ~~already~~ read the book.

A **Rewrite each statement or question with <u>already</u> or <u>yet</u>.**

1. (yet) Has she finished the book? _____?

2. (yet) They haven't seen the movie. _____.

3. (already) We've tried wild rice several times. _____.

4. (already) Has your father left _____?

B **Rewrite each sentence with <u>already</u> or <u>yet</u>.**

1. I haven't had dinner. _____.

2. She's been to London, Berlin, and Rome. _____.

3. They haven't called home. _____.

4. We've finished our class. _____.

The present perfect: <u>ever</u>, <u>never</u>, and <u>before</u>

Use <u>ever</u> in questions. Do not use <u>ever</u> in affirmative statements.

Have you **ever** made sushi?	Yes, I have. OR Yes, I've made it.
	(NOT Yes, I've ~~ever~~ made it.)

Use <u>never</u> in negative short answers and statements.

Have you ever made sushi?	No, I **never** have.
	OR No, I've **never** made sushi.

You can use <u>before</u> with or without <u>ever</u> and <u>never</u> in present perfect sentences and questions.

  I've been to South Africa **before**.
  I've **never** tried ceviche **before**.
  Have you **ever** made chocolate cake **before**?

In very informal speech, <u>ever</u> is sometimes used to strongly emphasize <u>never</u>. The meaning of <u>ever</u> is similar to "in my whole life."

  I've **never ever** made sushi!

C> **Answer the questions, using real information. If the answer is <u>yes</u>, write when this happened.**

1. Have you ever gone on a cruise? _____.

2. Have you ever tried Indian food? _____.

3. Have you ever been to Hawaii? _____.

4. Have you ever met a famous person? _____.

5. Have you ever gone scuba diving? _____.

▶ UNIT 2   Lesson 1

┌─ **The present perfect and the present perfect continuous: unfinished actions** ─

Unfinished actions are those that began in the past, continue in the present, and may continue into the future. Here are three ways to talk about unfinished (or continuous) actions:

1. the present perfect with <u>since</u>: Use <u>since</u> with a stated start time in the past.
   I've lived here **since** 2001. (2001 is the stated start time. I still live here.)

2. the present perfect with <u>for</u>: Use <u>for</u> to describe the period of time from its start until the present.
   I've lived here **for** five years. (Emphasis is on the five-year period. I still live here.)

3. the present perfect continuous with <u>for</u> and <u>since</u>: Form the present perfect continuous with the present perfect of <u>be</u> and a present participle.
   I've been living here since 2001. OR **I've been living** here for five years.

A> **Complete each statement with the present perfect continuous.**

1. *Seabiscuit* _____ at the Park Lane Classic Cinema since April.
   play

2. Robert _____ in the ticket holders' line for a pretty long time.
   wait

3. People _____ violence in movies since the sixties.
   worry about

4. I _____ that movie with everyone for weeks.
   talk about

5. We _____ to this movie theater for two years.
   come

B> **Read the sentences. Check if the sentence describes an unfinished (continuous) action. Then rewrite those sentences in the present perfect continuous.**

☐ 1. The Grants have lived in Buenos Aires since the late seventies.

☐ 2. Their friends have already visited them.

☐ 3. We have waited to see you for three years.

☐ 4. This is the first time I've visited Paris.

☐ 5. We have eaten in that great Indian restaurant for years.

☐ 6. Has she ever met your teacher?

☐ 7. How long have you studied Chinese?

☐ 8. My children have just come back from the movies.

C **Write the present participle for the following base forms.**

1. find _____
2. be _____
3. lose _____
4. put _____
5. get _____
6. say _____
7. write _____
8. go _____
9. make _____
10. fix _____
11. know _____

12. speak _____
13. hear _____
14. let _____
15. come _____
16. leave _____
17. drive _____
18. meet _____
19. blow _____
20. give _____
21. run _____
22. forget _____

23. eat _____
24. pay _____
25. stand _____
26. think _____
27. buy _____
28. see _____
29. begin _____
30. tell _____
31. bring _____
32. take _____

Will and be going to

Use will or be going to for predictions about the future. The meaning is the same.

> It'll rain tomorrow.
> It's going to rain tomorrow.

Use be going to when you already have a plan for the future.

> A: Are you going to come to class tomorrow?
> B: No, I'm going to go to the beach instead.

Use will to talk about the immediate future when you do not already have a plan.

> Maybe I'll go to the beach this weekend.

Use will for willingness.

> I'll eat meat, but I won't eat vegetables.

A **Write five sentences about your plans for this weekend.**

_____.

_____.

_____.

_____.

_____.

B **Write five sentences using will for willingness on one of the following topics: types of exercise you are willing to do; types of food you are willing to eat for breakfast; types of clothes you are NOT willing to wear.**

_____.

_____.

_____.

_____.

_____.

┌─ **Degrees of obligation** ────────────────────────────────

have to / must

Use <u>have to</u> (OR <u>have got to</u>) or <u>must</u>* to express obligation. These modals suggest there is no other choice of action available.

> Students **must** take this exam to graduate.
> If you want to arrive before 8:00, you **have to** (OR **have got to**) take the 6:00 train.

had better

Use <u>had better</u> to mean there is a consequence for not doing something.

> You'**d better** make a reservation. The hotel is very popular.

be supposed to

Use <u>be supposed to</u> to mean that other people expect you to take this action.

> We're **supposed** to check out by twelve, but I think we can get a late checkout if we ask.

should / ought to†

Use <u>should</u> or <u>ought to</u> to state an opinion or give advice.

> You **should** (OR **ought to**) stay at the Milton Hotel. It's close to town and very good.

could

Use <u>could</u> to suggest an alternative action.

> They **could** stay at the Festival Hotel if there are no rooms at the Milton.

BE CAREFUL!

In the negative, <u>must not</u> (OR <u>mustn't</u>) expresses a prohibition.

> You **must not** smoke here. = Don't smoke here.

However, <u>don't have to</u> expresses a lack of obligation.

> You **don't have to** show your passport to cash a check.

* <u>Must</u> is very formal and is likely to be used by a person in authority (a teacher to students, for example). <u>Have got to</u> is often used in spoken English with the same meaning as <u>have to</u>.

† <u>Ought to</u> has the same meaning as <u>should</u>, but is slightly less formal. Don't use <u>ought to</u> in questions or negative statements.

───

 Choose the sentence closer in meaning to each numbered statement or question.

1. Do you think the Milton Hotel is a good place to stay?

   a. Do you think I should stay at the Milton?
   b. Do you think I have to stay at the Milton?

2. If you don't have your luggage ticket, the bellman won't give you your luggage.

   a. You could give the bellman the ticket.
   b. You must give the bellman the ticket.

3. They don't accept credit cards in this hotel. They only accept cash.

   a. You have to pay with cash.
   b. You'd better pay with cash.

4. When I made the reservation, I asked for a suite.

    a. They mustn't give me a suite.
    b. They're supposed to give me a suite.

5. Don't wear shorts in the restaurant.

    a. You must not wear shorts in the restaurant.
    b. You don't have to wear shorts in the restaurant.

UNIT 4   *Lesson 1*

The past continuous: uses

The past continuous describes an action that was continuous until (and possibly after) the moment at which another action took place. The words <u>when</u> or <u>while</u> are often used with the past continuous.

    He **was talking** on the phone when the storm began.
    While I **was living** in Chile, I got married.

The past continuous also describes two continuing actions occurring in the same period of time.

    While she **was driving**, her husband **was reading** the newspaper.
    They **were eating**, and the music **was playing**.

The past continuous is also used when we report someone else's words.

    They said, "We are arriving at three o'clock."   →   They said they **were arriving** at three o'clock.

A **Write questions with the past continuous.**

1. (YOU) _____?

    "She was taking a test at school."

2. (YOU) _____?

    "I was talking to my mother on the phone."

3. (YOU) _____?

    "Mr. Kemp was driving."

4. (YOU) _____?

    "At three o'clock? The teacher was teaching an art class."

5. (YOU) _____?

    "I'm not sure. I think they were cooking."

UNIT 4   Lesson 2

Direct objects

Verbs are either transitive or intransitive. Transitive verbs have direct objects. In English sentences, direct object nouns and pronouns come after the verb.

   I love **my car**.   She bought **new tires**.   They painted **it**.

Many phrasal verbs are called "separable" because the direct object can come before or after the particle.

   They **dropped off** their car. They **dropped** their car **off**.

BUT: When the direct object is a pronoun, it must come before the particle.

   They **dropped** it **off**.   NOT They ~~dropped off~~ it.

subject pronouns	object pronouns
I	me
you	you
he	him
she	her
it	it
we	us
they	them

A **Complete the conversations with phrasal verbs and object pronouns.**

1. **A:** Can I drop the car off early?

   B: Yes, you can _____ before nine o'clock.

2. **A:** Don't forget to fill the car up with gas and get oil.

   B: Don't worry. I'll _____ after English class.

3. **A:** I don't know which switch turns on the headlights.

   B: _____ with this switch.

4. **A:** How do I turn the air-conditioning off? It's freezing in here.

   B: The air-conditioning? You can _____ with that switch over there.

5. **A:** I need to pick the car up soon. What time will it be ready?

   B: Let's see. It'll be ready at 4:00. Please _____ then.

UNIT 5   Lesson 1

Non-count nouns: containers, quantifiers, and other modifiers

REMEMBER: Count nouns name things you can count individually. They have singular and plural forms. Non-count nouns name things you cannot count individually. They don't have plural forms.

Containers, quantifiers, and other modifiers make non-count nouns countable.

   two kilos of rice   **three cups of** coffee

The following is a list of common containers and quantifiers:

a kilo	a gallon	a carton	a bottle	a cup
a gram	a liter	a package	a jar	a spoonful
a pound	a bag	a container	a tube	a slice
an ounce	a box	a can	a bar	a loaf

A Make each of these non-count nouns countable. Use quantifiers or container words.

1. rice _____

2. chocolate _____

3. milk _____

4. toothpaste _____

5. shampoo _____

6. shaving cream _____

7. body lotion _____

Too many, too much, and enough

The word <u>too</u> indicates a quantity that is excessive—more than someone wants or needs. Use <u>enough</u> to say if something is satisfactory.

Use <u>too many</u> (and <u>not too many</u>) for count nouns.

There are **too many customers** waiting in line.

Use <u>too much</u> (and <u>not too much</u>) for non-count nouns.

There's **too much toothpaste** on the toothbrush.

Use <u>enough</u> (and <u>not enough</u>) for both count and non-count nouns.

There's **enough shampoo**, but there aren't **enough razors**.

B Complete each sentence with <u>too many</u>, <u>too much</u>, or <u>enough</u>.

1. Let's make a nice dessert. Do we have _____ milk in the fridge?

2. This coffee has _____ sugar. It's awful.

3. It's not a good idea to buy _____ fruit. We're not going to be home for a few days.

4. This menu has _____ choices. I can't make up my mind.

5. Check the bathroom shelf to see if we have _____ soap. Mom and Dad are coming to visit.

6. I don't like when there are _____ brands. I can't decide which one to buy.

7. There's no way to get a haircut today. _____ people had the same idea!

8. I don't have _____ gas in the car for a long trip. Could you please get some when you go out?

9. They don't want to spend _____ money on their vacation. They're going camping.

UNIT 5   Lesson 2

Indefinite pronouns: <u>something</u>, <u>anything</u>, and <u>nothing</u>

Use <u>something</u> in affirmative statements.

There's **something** in this box.

Use <u>anything</u> in negative statements.

There **isn't anything** in the fridge.

Use <u>something</u> or <u>anything</u> in <u>yes</u> / <u>no</u> questions.

Is there **something** we should talk about? Is **anything** wrong?

<u>Nothing</u> is the equivalent of <u>not anything</u>. Don't use <u>nothing</u> in negative statements.

There isn't **anything** in the fridge. = There's **nothing** in the fridge.
NOT There ~~isn't nothing~~ in the fridge.

 Choose the correct indefinite pronoun to complete each sentence.

1. I need to go to the store to buy _____.
    something / anything

2. There is _____ I can do to help.
    something / anything

3. There isn't _____ you can do to make yourself taller.
    something / anything

4. A skin doctor can tell you _____ about how to use sunscreen.
    something / anything

5. They have _____ that helps you lose weight.
    something / anything

6. My dentist recommended _____ to whiten my teeth.
    something / anything

7. There's _____ that can make you look young again.
    anything / nothing

8. They can't get _____ to eat there after ten o'clock.
    anything / nothing

UNIT 6   Lesson 1

Negative <u>yes</u> / <u>no</u> questions: short answers

**Answer negative <u>yes</u> / <u>no</u> questions the same way as you would answer other
<u>yes</u> / <u>no</u> questions.**

Is Jane a vegetarian?
Isn't Jane a vegetarian?   } Yes, she is. / No, she isn't.

Do they have two sons?
Don't they have two sons?   } Yes, they do. / No, they don't.

A ▸ Read the information. Answer the negative question with a short answer.

1. (Hank is not a lawyer.)

    A: Isn't Hank a lawyer? **B:** _____.

2. (Bob has two younger brothers and an older sister.)

    A: Doesn't Bob have two younger brothers and an older sister? **B:** _____.

3. (You have never been to Siberia.)

    A: Haven't you been to Siberia before? **B:** _____.

4. (You're learning English right now.)

    A: Aren't you learning English right now? **B:** _____.

5. (Nancy didn't go to the movie theater last night.)

    A: Wasn't Nancy at the movie theater last night? **B:** _____.

Why don't …? / Why doesn't …?

Make suggestions with <u>Why don't …?</u> or <u>Why doesn't …?</u>

A: It's cold.	**B:** Why don't you put on a sweater?
A: The play's at 8:00.	**B:** Why don't we leave early?
A: My daughter has a toothache.	**B:** Why doesn't she see a dentist?

B ▸ Write a suggestion with <u>Why don't …?</u> or <u>Why doesn't …?</u> for each situation.

1. "I'm not feeling well."

    YOU _____.

2. "I'm in the mood for seafood."

    YOU _____.

3. "My teacher works very hard. He hasn't taken a vacation for a long time."

    YOU _____.

4. "My neighbor can't open her door. The key is stuck."

    YOU _____.

5. "It's such a beautiful day. I don't want to stay indoors."

    YOU _____.

> **Used to: form**
>
> **In questions and negative statements, <u>used to</u> becomes <u>use to</u>.**
>
> When you were a kid, **did** you **use to** like vegetables?
> When I was a kid, I **didn't use to** like vegetables. I only used to like candy.

A **Write a <u>yes</u> / <u>no</u> question for each statement.**

1. I used to go running every day.

   Did you use to go running every day?

2. There used to be a large tree in front of my house.

   _____

3. Mr. and Mrs. Palmer used to go dancing every weekend.

   _____

4. My grandmother used to put sugar in our orange juice.

   _____

5. Luke used to be very heavy.

   _____

B **On a separate sheet of paper, write each sentence with a negative or affirmative form of <u>used to</u>.**

1. Jason and Trish / get lots of exercise, but now they go swimming every day.

2. There / be a movie theater on Smith Street, but now there isn't.

3. Nobody / worry about fatty foods, but now most people do.

4. English / be an international language, but now everyone uses English to communicate around the world.

5. Women / wear pants, but now it's very common.

Gerunds and infinitives

A gerund (an **–ing** form of a verb) functions as a noun. Gerunds can be subjects, objects, or subject complements.

> **Painting** is my favorite leisure-time activity. (subject)
> I love **painting**. (direct object)
> I read a book about the history of **painting**. (object of the preposition <u>of</u>)
> My favorite activity is **painting**. (subject complement)

An infinitive (<u>to</u> + the base form of a verb) also functions as a noun.

> **To paint** well is a talent. (subject)
> I love **to paint**. (direct object)
> The only thing he likes is **to paint**. (subject complement)

A **Underline the gerunds and circle the infinitives in the following sentences.**

1. I love watching DVDs, and I like to sing too.

2. Avoiding sweets makes a healthy change in your diet.

3. The most important thing I do is cooking dinner for my children.

4. What's the point of inviting her to the movies?

5. They're always angry about our leaving the lights on late.

6. Last year I devoted myself to studying English.

Gerunds and infinitives after certain verbs

Certain verbs are followed by gerunds:
    avoid, can't help, can't stand, consider, discuss, dislike, enjoy, feel like, finish,
    (don't) mind, practice, quit, suggest.

Certain verbs are followed by infinitives:
    agree, be sure, choose, decide, expect, hope, learn, need, plan, promise, refuse,
    seem, want, wish, would like.

Other verbs can be followed by either a gerund or an infinitive:
    begin, continue, hate, like, love, prefer, start.

B **Complete each sentence with a gerund or an infinitive.**

Let me tell you something about my husband. He enjoys ____________ (1. get up) early and ____________ (2. run) in the park. He doesn't mind ____________ (3. go), even when the weather is bad. On the mornings when he doesn't feel like ____________ (4. exercise), he sleeps late. One day, I would like ____________ (5. join) him when he exercises.

I actually prefer ____________ (6. go) to bed late, and I love ____________ (7. read) until midnight. But now I plan ____________ (8. stop) that habit. From tomorrow on, I want ____________ (9. go) to sleep early, even though I hate ____________ (10. do) that. We talked about it, and I agreed ____________ (11. change) my daily routine and ____________ (12. go) running with him for one week.

UNIT 7 Lesson 2

Negative gerunds

A gerund can be made negative by using a negative word before it.

I like **not going** to bed too late.
They complained about **never having** enough time.

A **Complete the following paragraph with affirmative and negative gerunds.**

I really want to do something to improve my appearance and lose weight. First of all, I'm sick of ____________ (1. be) able to fit into my clothes. I want to go on a diet, but I'm afraid of ____________ (2. feel) hungry all the time. I can't complain about ____________ (3. stay) in shape because right now I spend every afternoon ____________ (4. ride) my bike. However, I do worry about ____________ (5. have) enough energy to exercise if I've had a few days of ____________ (6. get) enough to eat.

The passive voice: form

Many sentences can be written in both active voice or passive voice. Form the passive voice with a form of <u>be</u> and the past participle of the verb.

	ACTIVE VOICE	PASSIVE VOICE
simple present tense	Art collectors **buy** famous paintings all over the world.	Famous paintings **are bought by** art collectors all over the world.
present continuous	The Film Center **is showing** Kurosawa's films.	Kurosawa's films **are being shown** at the Film Center.
present perfect	World leaders **have bought** Yu Hung's paintings.	Yu Hung's paintings **have been bought** by world leaders.
simple past tense	I.M. Pei **designed** the Grand Pyramid at the Louvre.	The Grand Pyramid at the Louvre **was designed** by I.M. Pei.
past continuous	Last year, the museum **was selling** copies of Monet's paintings.	Last year, copies of Monet's paintings **were being sold** by the museum.
future with <u>will</u>	Ang Lee **will direct** a new film next year.	A new film **will be directed** by Ang Lee next year.
future with <u>be going to</u>	The Tate Gallery **is going to show** Van Gogh's *Sunflowers* next month.	Van Gogh's *Sunflowers* **is going to be shown** at the Tate Gallery next month.

The passive voice: use

The active voice focuses on the "doer" of the action. Use the passive voice to focus on the "receiver" of the action.

A Japanese art collector   bought   Van Gogh's portrait of Dr. Gachet.

Van Gogh's portrait of Dr. Gachet   was bought by   a Japanese art collector.

Use the passive voice when:

   a. the person or thing doing the action is not known or not important.

      Ceramic pottery **is made** in many parts of the world.

   b. the person or thing doing the action is clear from context.

      Frida Kahlo did a lot of painting after her accident. A number of her self-portraits **were painted** at that time.

The <u>by</u> phrase
Use a <u>by</u> phrase in passive voice sentences when it is important to know who is performing an action.

   The *Mona Lisa* was painted **by Leonardo Da Vinci**.   (important)
   This stone carving was found (~~by someone~~) in Costa Rica.   (not important)

The passive voice: intransitive verbs

Intransitive verbs don't have objects. With intransitive verbs, there is no "receiver" of an action. For that reason, intransitive verbs are not used in the passive voice.

John **arrives** tomorrow.　　Janet **came** to the party.　　We **live** in an apartment.

Some common intransitive verbs:

die	happen	rain	sleep	arrive	fall	laugh	
seem	stand	come	go	live	sit	stay	walk

 On a separate sheet of paper, rewrite the sentences that have transitive verbs, changing them from the active voice into the passive voice.

1. Pedro Almodóvar is directing a new film about women.

2. A Canadian art collector has bought two of Michelangelo's drawings.

3. Someone stole Edvard Munch's painting *The Scream* in 2004.

4. The painter Georgia O'Keeffe lived in the southwestern part of the United States for many years.

5. The Van Gogh Museum in Amsterdam will send *Sunflowers* on tour.

6. The British Museum has bought some new sculptures for its ancient Roman collection.

7. The Metropolitan Museum of Art is going to open a new gallery next year.

 On a separate sheet of paper, rewrite these sentences in the passive voice. Use a <u>by</u> phrase only if it is important to know who is performing the action.

1. Someone actually stole the *Mona Lisa* in 1911.

2. Paloma Picasso designed these pieces of jewelry.

3. People built great pyramids throughout Central America during the height of the Mayan civilization.

4. Someone will repair the sculpture when it gets old.

5. People have paid millions of U.S. dollars for Van Gogh's paintings.

6. Hmong people from Laos made this colorful cloth.

UNIT 8 Lesson 2

The passive voice: questions

To form yes / no questions in the passive voice, move the first auxiliary verb before the subject.

simple present tense	**Are** famous paintings ~~are~~ **bought** by art collectors?
present continuous	**Are** Kurosawa's films ~~are~~ **being shown** at the Film Center?
present perfect	**Have** Yu Hung's paintings ~~have~~ **been bought** by world leaders?
simple past tense	**Was** the Grand Pyramid at the Louvre ~~was~~ designed by I.M. Pei?
past continuous	**Were** copies of Monet's paintings ~~were~~ **being sold** by the museum?
future with will	**Will** a new film ~~will~~ **be directed** by Ang Lee next year?
future with be going to	**Is** Van Gogh's *Sunflowers* ~~is~~ **going to be shown** at the Tate Gallery next month?

  On a separate sheet of paper, rewrite the sentences as yes / no questions in the passive voice.

1. That new film about families is being directed by Gillian Armstrong.

2. One of Da Vinci's most famous drawings has been sold by a German art collector.

3. A rare ceramic figure from the National Palace Museum in Taipei will be sent to the Metropolitan Museum of Art in New York.

4. A new exhibit is going to be opened at the Photography Gallery this week.

5. Some new paintings have been bought by the Prado Museum for their permanent collection.

6. *Las Meninas* can be seen at the Prado Museum in Madrid.

7. The *Jupiter* Symphony was written by Mozart.

8. Some of Michelangelo's work was being shown around the world in the 1960s.

UNIT 9 Lesson 1

Comparison with adjectives: review

Comparatives

Use comparatives to show how two things are different in degree.

> My laptop is **lighter than** John's (is).

Superlatives

Use superlatives to show how one thing is different from two or more other things.

> The M12, LX, and Pell monitors are all good monitors. But the Pell is **the best**.

as ... as

Use as ... as to show that two things are equal. Use the negative form to show that two things are different.

> The new X12 monitor is **as big as** the old X10 model. (They're the same size.)
> The Perk monitor is **not as big as** the X12. (They're of different sizes.)

Each sentence has one error. Correct the error.

1. The Ortman headset isn't as clear~~er~~ as the Pike headset.

2. My old laptop didn't have as many problems than my new laptop.

3. I checked out the three top brands, and the Piston was definitely the better.

4. Maxwell's web camera is much more expensive as their digital camera.

5. Of all the monitors I looked at, the X60 is definitely larger.

As … as with adverbs

Adverbs often give information about verbs
> My phone works **well**.   My printer prints **fast**.

Many adjectives can be changed to adverbs by adding –ly.
> loud → loud**ly**   bad → bad**ly**
>
> poor → poor**ly**   quiet → quiet**ly**
>
> quick → quick**ly**   slow → slow**ly**

You can use as … as with many adverbs.
> My new phone works **as well as** my old one.
> The Macro laptop doesn't run **as slowly as** the Pell laptop.

 Read the statements. On a separate sheet of paper, write sentences with as … as.

1. My brother's MP3 player downloads quickly. My MP3 player also downloads quickly.

2. My new computer doesn't log on slowly. My old computer logs on slowly.

3. Your scanner works well. My scanner also works well.

4. The Rico printer prints quickly. The Grant printer doesn't print quickly.

5. The Pax CD drive doesn't run quietly. The Rico CD drive runs quietly.

UNIT 9   *Lesson 2*

Expressing purpose with in order to

You can use in order to to express purpose. The following three sentences have the same meaning:
> I scrolled down **because I wanted to** read the text.
> I scrolled down **in order to** read the text.
> I scrolled down **to** read the text.

On a separate sheet of paper, rewrite the sentences with <u>in order to</u>.

1. I joined a chat room to meet new people.

2. Jason surfs the Internet to find interesting websites.

3. Alison is instant messaging her friend Nancy to invite her for dinner.

4. They always print their files to read them.

5. I never use the pull-down menu to open a file.

Expressing purpose with <u>for</u>

You can use <u>for</u> to express purpose. Use <u>for</u> before a noun.

> She e-mailed me **for some advice.**
> They shop online **for electronics products**.

Never use <u>for</u> before an infinitive of purpose.

> DON'T SAY She e-mailed me ~~for~~ to ask a question.

 Complete each sentence with <u>for</u> or <u>to</u>.

1. My friend Jay e-mailed me _____ say he's getting married.

2. Matt created a web page _____ keep in touch with his family and friends.

3. I went online _____ find a new keyboard.

4. Jane shops online _____ clothing.

5. When Gina's computer crashed, her brother came to her apartment _____ help her.

6. Sometimes I use my computer _____ download music.

7. I designed a new home page _____ my company.

8. We both log on to the Internet _____ information.

UNIT 10 Lesson 2

Conditional sentences: meaning

Conditional sentences express a result of an action. They usually have an <u>if</u> clause and a result clause.

if clause (the condition)	result clause
If I eat dinner at home,	I don't eat too much.
If they speak Dutch to the taxi driver,	he won't understand.
If they had more money,	they would take a trip.

Underline the result clause in each of the following sentences.

1. If the weather is good, I exercise outside.

2. I'm not happy if I don't get enough sleep.

3. If they were extroverts, they would talk more.

4. The students will start on Monday if they get their books in time.

Conditional sentences: present factual

Use the present factual conditional to talk about general and scientific facts. Use the simple present tense or the present tense of <u>be</u> in both clauses.

If it **rains**, flights **are** delayed. (general fact)
If you **heat** water to 100 degrees, it **boils**. (scientific fact)

B **Complete each present factual conditional sentence.**

1. Water _____ if you _____ its temperature below 0 degrees.
             freeze   lower

2. If I _____ something on the ground in the street, I _____ it to the owner.
    see   return

3. She _____ on vacation in August if she _____ too much work.
       go   not have

4. He _____ in the park if the weather _____ dry.
      run   be

Conditional sentences: future factual

Use the future factual conditional to talk about what will happen in the future under certain conditions. Use the simple present tense in the <u>if</u> clause. Use the future with <u>will</u> or <u>be going to</u> in the result clause.

If I **go** to sleep too late tonight, I **won't be able to get up** on time. (future condition, future result)
If she **comes** home after 8:00, I'm **not going to make** dinner. (future condition, future result)

Don't use a future form in the <u>if</u> clause.

If I **see** him, I'll tell him. NOT If I ~~will~~ see him, I'll tell him.
                          NOT If I ~~'m going to~~ see him, I'll tell him.

C **Choose the correct form to complete each future factual conditional sentence.**

1. If they _____ the movie, they _____ it again.
              like / will like   see / will see

2. I _____ to her if she _____ that again.
    'm going to talk / talk   does / 's going to do

3. If you _____ some eggs, I _____ you an omelet tonight.
      buy / are going to buy   make / 'll make

4. If they _____ her tomorrow, they _____ her home.
      see /will see   drive / 'll drive

5. _____ Italian if they _____ it next year?
    Are you going to study / Do you study   offer / will offer

Conditional sentences: present unreal

Use the present unreal conditional to talk about unreal conditions and their results. Use the simple past tense in the _if_ clause. For the verb _be_, always use _were_. Use _would_ and a base form in the result clause.

> If I **had** black shoes, I **would wear** them. (But I don't have black shoes: unreal condition, unreal result.)
> If I **were** a teacher, I **would teach** French. (But I'm not a teacher: unreal condition, unreal result.)

Don't use _would_ in the _if_ clause.

> If I **knew** his name, I would tell you. NOT If I ~~would know~~ his name, I would tell you.

 Complete each present unreal conditional sentence. Use your _own_ ideas.

1. If I lived to be 100, _____.

2. My family would be angry if _____.

3. If I didn't study English, _____.

4. If I went to my favorite restaurant, _____.

5. If I were a child again, _____.

6. The English class would be better if _____.

Conditional sentences: order of clauses

In all conditional sentences, the clauses can be reversed with no change in meaning. In writing, use a comma between the clauses when the _if_ clause comes first.

> If you don't return the bracelet, you'll feel bad.
> You'll feel bad if you don't return the bracelet.

E **On a separate sheet of paper, rewrite all the sentences in exercises A–D, reversing the clauses and using commas where necessary.**

🎧 TOP NOTCH POP LYRICS 🎵

Greetings and Small Talk [Unit 1]

You look so familiar. Have we met before?
I don't think you're from around here.
It might have been two weeks ago, but I'm not sure.
Has it been a month or a year?
I have a funny feeling that I've met you twice.
That's what they call déjà vu.
You were saying something friendly, trying to be nice,
and now you're being friendly too.
One look, one word.
It's the friendliest sound that I've ever heard.
Thanks for your greeting.
I'm glad this meeting occurred.

(CHORUS)
Greetings and small talk
make the world go round.
On every winding road I've walked,
this is what I've found.

Have you written any letters to your friends back home?
Have you had a chance to do that?
Have you spoken to your family on the telephone?
Have you taken time for a chat?
Bow down, shake hands.
Do whatever you do in your native land.
I'll be happy to greet you
in any way that you understand.

(CHORUS)

Have you seen the latest movie out of Hollywood?
Have you read about it yet?
If you haven't eaten dinner, are you in the mood
for a meal you won't forget?
Bow down, shake hands.
Do whatever you do in your native land.
I'll be happy to greet you
in any way that you understand.

(CHORUS)

Better Late Than Never [Unit 2]

Where have you been? I've waited for you.
I'd rather not say how long.
The movie began one hour ago.
How did you get the time all wrong?
Well, I got stuck in traffic, and when I arrived,
I couldn't find a parking place.
Did you buy the tickets? You're kidding—for real?
Let me pay you back, in that case.

(CHORUS)
Sorry I'm late.
I know you've waited here forever.
How long has it been?
It's always better late than never.

When that kind of movie comes to the big screen,
it always attracts a crowd.
And I've always wanted to see it with you,
but it looks like we've missed it now.
I know what you're saying, but actually,
I would rather watch a video.
So why don't we rent it and bring it back home?
Let's get in the car and go.

(CHORUS)
Didn't you mention, when we made our plans,
that you've seen this movie recently?
It sounds so dramatic, and I'm so upset,
I'd rather see a comedy!
Well, which comedy do you recommend?
It really doesn't matter to me.
I still haven't seen *The World and a Day*.
I've heard that one is pretty funny.

(CHORUS)

Wheels around the World [Unit 4]

Was I going too fast
or a little too slow?
I was looking out the window,
and I just don't know.
I must have turned the steering wheel
a little too far
when I drove into the bumper
of that luxury car.
Oh no!
How awful!
What a terrible day!
I'm sorry to hear that.
Are you OK?

(CHORUS)
Wheels around the World
are waiting here with your car.
Pick it up.
Turn it on.
Play the radio.
Wheels around the World—
"helping you to go far."
You can drive anywhere.
Buckle up and go.

Did I hit the red sedan,
or did it hit me?
I was talking on the cell phone
in my SUV.
Nothing was broken,
and no one was hurt,
but I did spill some coffee
on my favorite shirt.
Oh no!
Thank goodness
you're still alive!
I'm so happy that
you survived.

(CHORUS)
What were you doing when you hit that tree?
I was racing down the mountain, and the brakes failed me.
How did it happen? Was the road still wet?
Well, there might have been a danger sign, but I forget.
The hood popped open and the door fell off.
The headlights blinked and the engine coughed.
The side-view mirror had a terrible crack.
The gearshift broke. Can I bring the car back?
Oh no!
Thank goodness
you're still alive!
I'm so happy that
you survived.

(CHORUS)

The Colors of Love [Unit 7]

Are you sick and tired of working hard day and night?
Do you like to look at the world in shades of black and white?
Your life can still be everything that you were dreaming of.
Just take a look around you and see all the colors of love.
You wake up every morning and go through the same old grind.
You don't know how the light at the window could be so unkind.
If blue is the color that you choose when the road is rough,
you know you really need to believe in the colors of love.

(CHORUS)
The colors of love
are as beautiful as a rainbow.
The colors of love
shine on everyone in the world.

Are negative thoughts and emotions painful to express?
They're just tiny drops in the ocean of happiness.
And these are the feelings you must learn to rise above.
Your whole life is a picture you paint with the colors of love.

(CHORUS)

To Each His Own [Unit 8]

He doesn't care for Dali.
The colors are too bright.
He says that Picasso
got everything just right.
She can't stand the movies
that are filmed in Hollywood.
She likes Almodóvar.
She thinks he's really good.
He's inspired by everything
she thinks is second-rate.
She's moved and fascinated
by the things he loves to hate.
He's crazy about art that only
turns her heart to stone.
I guess that's why they say
to each his own.
He likes pencil drawings.
She prefers photographs.
He takes her to the art museum,
but she just laughs and laughs.
He loves the Da Vinci
that's hanging by the door.
She prefers the modern art
that's lying on the floor.
"No kidding! You'll love it. Just wait and see.
It's perfect in every way."
She shakes her head. "It's not for me.
It's much too old and gray."
She thinks he has the worst taste
that the world has ever known.
I guess that's why they say
to each his own.
But when it's time to say good-bye,
they both feel so alone.
I guess that's why they say
to each his own.